Linux Comman

The fast and easy beginner's guide to learn Linux basics in 7 easy steps.

[Steve Eddison]

Legal & Disclaimer

The information contained in this book and its contents is not designed to replace or take the place of any form of medical or professional advice; and is not meant to replace the need for independent medical, financial, legal or other professional advice or services, as may be required. The content and information in this book have been provided for educational and entertainment purposes only.

The content and information contained in this book has been compiled from sources deemed reliable, and it is accurate to the best of the Author's knowledge, information and belief. However, the Author cannot guarantee its accuracy and validity and cannot be held liable for any errors and/or omissions. Further, changes are periodically made to this book as and when needed. Where appropriate and/or necessary, you must consult a professional (including but not limited to your doctor, attorney, financial advisor or such other professional advisor) before using any of the suggested remedies, techniques, or information in this book.

Upon using the contents and information contained in this book, you agree to hold harmless the Author from and against any damages, costs, and expenses, including any legal fees potentially resulting from the application of any of the information provided by this book. This disclaimer applies to any loss, damages or injury caused by the use and application, whether directly or indirectly, of any advice or information presented, whether for breach of contract, tort, negligence, personal injury, criminal intent, or under any other cause of action.

You agree to accept all risks of using the information presented inside this book.

You agree that by continuing to read this book, where appropriate and/or necessary, you shall consult a professional (including but not limited to your doctor, attorney, or financial advisor or such other advisor as needed) before using any of the suggested remedies, techniques, or information in this book.

Table of Contents

Introduction **7**

Command line basics 12

Opening a Terminal 12

What is your location? 16

Absolute and Relative Paths 18

Tab Completion 22

Chapter 1. Getting started **24**

Choosing the Right Linux Distributor 37

Chapter 2. Linux installation **42**

Post-Installation Activities 50

Chapter 3. Linux application **57**

Where to Get Apps? 57

Office Tools and Applications 58

Using Multimedia Apps 60

Using Digital Cameras with Linux 60

How to Play Audio from a CD 62

How to Play Sound Files 63

How to Burn a Disc In Linux 64

Graphics and Imaging Apps 64

The GIMP 65

GNOME Ghostview.......................... 66

Chapter 4. Becoming a Linux power user 67

'Group' Commands.......................... 67

Chapter 5. Using the Shell 79

Environment Variables . **Errore. Il segnalibro non**
è definito.

Chapter 6. How to use Linux desktop 92

Desktop Panels 92

Use an Integrated Development Environment .. 104

Write Patches 105

Chapter 7. Working with the Command Line 110

essential Linux commands........................ 116

net-tools.................................... 149

Echo...................................... 149

Cat.. 150

Nano, jed, vi................................ 150

Df 152

Tar 153

Zip and unzip 153

Uname 153

Apt-get 154

Chmod 155

Hostname 156

Ping 156

iotop , iftop, hotp 157

Understanding processes 166

Chapter 8. Tips and Tricks 177

Creating a Directory 177

Removing a Directory 180

Moving a File or Directory 185

Renaming Files and Directories 187

Removing a File (and Non-Empty Directories) .. 188

A Command Line Editor 189

Saving and Exiting 192

Conclusion 194

Introduction

Congratulations on purchasing *Linux Command Line* and thank you for doing so.

When you take a look at the Linux, it is imperative to try and look back at its evolution. Despite being one of the most powerful operating systems today, Linux had very humble beginnings, and below is the history of how it came to be.

<u>Humble Beginnings</u>

In 1969, Unix came to life, thanks to Ken Thompson and Dennis Ritchie. From that, several projects came up in the eighties based on Unix, trying to take it a step further. Projects such as BSD, The Book Operating Systems and MINIX all came up during this time. All this was water under the bridge until a bright Finnish student by the name of Linus Torvalds combined the knowledge he had about the previous system and came up with a Kernel that would later take the world by storm.

1991 is the true birth of Linux. Linus created a free terminal emulator based on MINIX, and he named his version Freax. Although he did not want it called Linux since it would have seemed egoistic, a friend of his renamed the version that had been uploaded to an FTP server for future development Linux and thus the name was born.

The Desktop Linux

The period between 1992 and 1994 saw the growth of the desktop founders. Slackware, Debian and Red Hat Linux were released during this period with Linux kernel version 0.95 that was able to run on the X Window System. Although Slackware's start was filled with many challenges, it became the first Linux distribution to support the 0.99 kernel version as well as TCP/IP stack. However, the release of Linux 1.0.0 in March 1994 was the game changer. This version boasted of 176, 250 lines of code, something that was extraordinary at this time.

The Launch of Gnome and KDE

The next chapter on the history of Linux took place between 1995 and 1999. Jurix Linux came out during this time, and it is believed to be the first Linux distribution to support bootp and NFS. It was possible to copy an installed version onto a similar machine. It is this distro that set the platform for the

SUSE Linux that we know today. The Red Hat branch was not left behind. Within these five years, it had spearheaded the evolution of the Linux kernel from version 1.2.0 to 2.2. This pre-millennium era also saw a huge improvement in memory management and support for PowerPC architecture come to life. This was also when Linux started gaining popularity as the server OS of choice amongst IT professionals.

Other notable developments within this period were the establishment of the KDE and Gnome environments. KDE was founded by Matthias Ettrich, then a student at the University of Tübingen. On the other hand, Red Hat had evolved into the Gnome environment. While all these changes were happening, Sun and Oracle announced official support for the different versions of Linux.

Live Distributions

The next five years after the millennium hype saw the rise of some amazing things in the Linux family. Many Linux powered computers came to light, and the kernel also underwent a lot of changes. Heaps of new applications were developed and above all, the first live distro came to life.

Knoppix was popular between 2000 and 2005 because it could boot directly from CD. This happened in 2000 and set the bar high enough for other Linux distros. It is also imperative to note that Linux has also started losing its originality and looking more and more like Microsoft operating systems. This prompted the formation of the Linux Foundation to ensure that it regained its freedom and independence.

Another notable milestone during this period was the release of Linux kernel version 2.4 which had support for USB, PC cards, EXT3 file system, RAID, Bluetooth and PnP capabilities. Semantics are the set of rules that determine the meaning of instructions written in a programming language. While syntax is checked by the interpreter at the time of execution of the program, mistakes in the semantics of the program are usually harder to detect. To avoid semantic mistakes, it is advised to spend time on planning and analysis of the problem before starting to code it. If planned properly, the program will have fewer logical and semantical mistakes and thus the implementation will take much less time.

An example of mistake in the semantics of the language is when we calculate the mean of different numbers. Instead of dividing the sum of numbers with the (total number) if we divide it with (total number)-1 the result would be wrong but the interpreter would not show any errors because it does not understand the semantics of the programs, the programmer has to take care of it.

Now let us take a look at various parts of a Python program. Unlike compiler-based languages, an interpreter-based language does not need a complete program before it can parse it. It can take a single line of code and interpret it for the computer.

This kernel was so powerful that it became the longest supported one, ending with the release of 2.4.37.11 in 2011. Further updates to 2.6 saw the support for more CPUs, 16TB filesystem sizes and EXT4.

The Ubuntu Era

After 2005, things had started to stabilize, and this led to what came to be known as the Ubuntu era of 2006 to 2012. Linux Mint, today's most popular Ubuntu based distro was released in 2006. This era was mainly coupled with changes in the KDE with version 4.0 getting a lot of criticism. However, KDE 4.2 that was later released in 2009 fixed many of the issues of its predecessor. The Ubuntu era coincided with what is going to be or already is the largest Linux-based operating system, Android.

The Future

Today, Linux boasts of over 22 million users and Linux Mint has remained one of the most popular distributions. Although the beginnings can have been small, the future still holds a lot for Linux and only time will tell.

Command line basics

Opening a command line is simple. I can't exactly tell you how it is done because each system is different however below are some places to begin looking.

Opening a Terminal

If you are using Linux, then you will get it in the Application - > System or Application- > Utilities. Also, you can 'right-click' on the computer and there will be an option 'Open in Terminal.'

If you are on Windows and wish to log remotely into another machine, you will require an SSH client. A rather perfect one is Putty.

The Shell, Bash

Within a command line, we have a shell. Which is a part of the operating system which defines how the terminal will look and behave after executing or running commands for you? There are different shells available however the most common one is referred to as bash which means Bourne again shell. I will assume that you are utilizing bash as your shell.

If you wish to know the type shell that you are utilizing, you can use a command called echo to show a system variable showing your current shell. Echo is a type of a command utilized to display messages.

echo $SHELL

/bin/bash

Provided that it prints something on the screen that ends in bash then everything is good.

Shortcuts

The command line can appear daunting, however, don't fret. Linux has a lot of shortcuts to make your life simple. Take note of each of them as they not only make your life simple but also, they will always save you from making mistakes like typos.

The first shortcut is, when you type commands, they are stored in a history. You are able to traverse this history utilizing the up and down arrow keys on your keyboard. Semantics are the set of rules that determine the meaning of instructions written in a programming language. While syntax is checked by the interpreter at the time of execution of the program, mistakes in the semantics of the program are usually harder to detect. To avoid semantic mistakes, it is advised to spend time on planning and analysis of the problem before starting to code it. If planned properly, the program will have fewer logical and semantical mistakes and thus the implementation will take much less time.

An example of mistake in the semantics of the language is when we calculate the mean of different numbers. Instead of dividing the sum of numbers with the (total number) if we divide it with (total number)-1 the result would be wrong but the interpreter would not show any errors because it does not understand the semantics of the programs, the programmer has to take care of it.

Now let us take a look at various parts of a Python program. Unlike compiler-based languages, an interpreter-based language does not need a complete program before it can parse it. It can take a single line of code and interpret it for the computer.

So, it is not a must that you have to type the whole command again, you can simply hit the up arrow a bit. Also, you are able to edit those commands utilizing the left and right arrow keys to move the cursor to the desired part.

In this part, we will look the basic of moving around the system. Some tasks rely on being in a position to find them. As such, this stuff actually forms the basis of being able to work efficiently in Linux. Ensure that you understand it better.

So, where are we?

The initial command we are going to look at is pwd which means Print Working Directory. Some commands in Linux will be abbreviated; this makes it easier to memorize them. This command does that. It informs you what your present directory is. Try it now.

Pwd

/home/mike

Some commands on the terminal will depend on you being in the correct location. As you are moving around, it can be simple to lose track of your location. Utilize this command always so as to know where you are.

What is your location?

It is good to know where you are. Next you will wish to know what is there. The command for this work is Is. It's short form for list. Let's try it.

Is

bin Docs public-html

pwd is run by itself without arguments. Is is more powerful. We have run it without any arguments in this case it will show a list of that location.

Is [set of options] [file system location]

In the example above, the square brackets imply that those items are options; we can rum the command with or without them.

Let's break it down:

Line 1 – is the basis form. It shows the content of our present directory.

Line 4 – is an individual command line option which shows that we are going to do a long listing which has the following:

First character shows whether the file or directory is normal.

Next nine characters are permissions for the directory or file.

The next is the number of blocks.

The next field shows the owner of the file.

The next is the group where the file belongs.

Next is the file size.

Following up is the file modification time.

Finally, is the file name.

Line 10 – is the command line argument. This tells us about the files contents.

Line 13 – is both an argument and a command line option. It did a long listing of the file.

Lines 12 and 18 - shows that we have just cut some of the commands usual output for brevities sake.

Paths

Paths are important in being proficient with Linux. When we refer to a directory or file on the command line, we are referring to a path. A path is a way of finding a directory or file on the system.

Absolute and Relative Paths

Absolute paths specify the location of a directory or file about the main directory. You can easily identify them as the begin with a/

Relative paths specify the location of a directory or file about where we are presently in the system.

Below is an example to illustrate:

Pwd

/home/mike

ls Docs

Myfile1.txt myfile2.txt myfile3.txt

...

ls/home/mike/Docs

myfile1.txt myfile2.txt myfile3.txt

...

Line 1 – we run pwd to show where we are present.

Line 4 – we ran ls offering it with a relative path.

Line 7 – we ran ls offering it with an absolute path.

More on paths

Below are more building blocks you can utilize to build your paths:

- (tilde) – it is a shortcut for your home directory.

. (dot) – it refers to your present directory.

.. (dot dot) – it refers to the main directory.

Below are some examples:

pwd

/home/mike

ls -/Docs

myfile1.txt myfile2.txt myfile3.txt

...

ls./Docs

myfile1.txt myfile2.txt myfile3.txt

...

ls../../

bin boot dev etc. home lib var

...

ls/

bin boot dev etc. home lib var

...

After trying around these on the terminal yourself, they will begin to make more sense. Ensure you understand how all these elements of constructing a path work.

Let's move around a bit

We utilize a command called cd (change directory) when we want to move around in the system. It works as follows.

cd [file system location]

When you run the command cd with no arguments, it will usually take you back to the home directory. The cd can run without a location as we show early in the shortcuts above however it will always run with an individual terminal argument which is the location we wish to shift to. Below are some examples:

pwd

/home/mike

cd Docs

ls

myfile1.txt myfile2.txt myfile3.txt

...

cd /

pwd

/

ls

bin boot dev etc home lib var

...

cd-/Docs

pwd

/home/mike/Docs

cd../../

pwd

/home

Cd

Pwd

/home/mike

Tab Completion

Writing out these paths can be challenging. Tab Completion is a mechanism that the command line poses that will assist you in this situation.

It is hard to demonstrate here so it is better if you try it out yourself. If you begin typing cd/hTab/Tab you will probably get a feel how it works.

Summary:

pwd

Print Working Directory.

ls

 List the content of a file.

cd

Change Directories.

Relative Path

A directory or file location compared to where you are presently on the system.

Absolute Path

A directory or file in relation to the root of the file system.

Chapter 1. Getting started

As for the preparation of disk space, this is the most crucial moment in the whole process of installing Linux. The fact is that if you install the system on a computer whose hard disk already has any data, then it is here that you should be careful not to accidentally lose it. If you install a Linux system on a "clean" computer or at least on a new hard disk, where there is no data, then everything is much simpler.

Why can't you install Linux in the same partition where you already have, for example, Windows, even with enough free space?

The fact is that Windows uses the FAT32 file system (in old versions – FAT16) or NTFS (in Windows NT / 2000), and in Linux, a completely different system called Extended File System 2 (ext2fs, in the newest versions – journaling extSfs). These file systems can be located only on different partitions of the hard disk.

Note that in Linux, physical hard disks are referred to as the first is hda, the second is hdb, the third is hdc, and so on (hdd, hde, hdf...).

Sometimes in the installation program of the system you can see the full names of the disks - / dev / hda instead of hda, / dev / hdb instead of hdb, and so on – this is the same thing for us now. The logical partitions of each disk are numbered. So, on a hda physical disk, there are hda1, hda2, and so on, hdb can be hdb1, hdb2, and so on. Do not be confused by the fact that these figures sometimes go in a row. It does not matter to us.

How to start installing Linux from disk

To begin installing Linux, insert the system CD into the drive and restart the computer by selecting the boot from CD. If you plan to install Linux over Windows, then the installation program can be run directly from it.

Moreover, if you are running Windows 95/98, the installation will start immediately, and if the installation program was launched from under a more powerful system, for example, Windows 2000, XP, Vista, Seven will still have to restart the computer from the CD disk.

Your computer may already be configured to boot from a CD. If the boot from the CD does not occur, when you restart your computer, enter the BIOS settings. On most systems, to do this, immediately after turning on the computer or restarting, press the Delete key or F11.

After that, find the Advanced BIOS Settings section. Sometimes the section name may be different, but in any case, it is very similar to that in this book. Enter it by first moving the pointer to it using the cursor keys and then pressing the Enter key. Now find in the parameters either the item Boot Sequence (boot order), or, if not, the item 1st boot device (first boot device). Use the cursor keys to select the desired item and, by changing its value using the Page Up and Page Down keys, make the first bootable CD-ROM device. Press the Esc key to exit the section, and then F10 to exit the BIOS with the saved settings. Most likely, the computer will ask you to confirm this intention. Usually, to confirm, you must press the Y key, which means yes.

All modern computers can boot from a CD. If for some reason your computer does not have this capability, you will have to create a boot diskette to install Linux. There are always special tools for this on the Linux distribution CD.

Usually, they are located in a folder called dos tools (or in a folder with a similar name). There are images of boot floppies and a DOS program for creating them. Read the README files on the distribution CD for more detailed instructions.

The installation of the Linux operating system can be divided into several stages:

disk space preparation;

selection of the programs (packages) you need;

device configuration and graphical interface;

install bootloader.

The installation program takes control of the entire process. You should only answer questions if the installation does not occur in fully automatic mode.

How to install Linux from a flash drive?

It often happens that if you want to install the OS, a person is faced with the fact that his drive is broken or missing. Especially often this problem happens with laptop owners. But do not be upset, because there is an alternative: installing from a Linux flash drive. To do this, you do not need a great deal of knowledge in programming, because there are special programs that "burn" the Linux image onto your USB flash drive just like on a disk. You will only need to start the installation process.

So, before you install Linux from a flash drive, you will need a flash drive with an image written onto it.

First, you should prepare the BIOS for installation.

As an example, consider installing a Linux Mint distribution. For the installation of Linux Mint from a flash drive to begin, you need to configure the startup parameters.

We insert the USB flash drive into the computer, turn it on at the very beginning, when there is a black screen on the screen and a lot of text, press the F2 button. Depending on the version of the BIOS and the computer, it may be another button – F10, Delete or Esc.

We get into the settings menu and now we need to find the "Boot" item. Again, in different versions of the BIOS it may be called differently but be guided by this word. After we have found the autorun menu, a list of priorities appears before our eyes. It contains: a hard disk, a disk drive, a removable hard disk, USB inputs, and so on. Our task is to find a flash drive in this list and put it in priority for 1 place.

It is done this way: we point the arrows at the name (for example: "USB 40GB DEVICE") and move it by pressing the F5 and F6 buttons until the USB flash drive is in 1st place.

Now the system will start the flash drive first. Press F10 and confirm the output by entering the Y (Yes) key and pressing the Enter button.

Reboot the computer.

After that you should start the installation process.

After the computer restarts, you will see the startup menu. Often it is decorated with various images, so you will understand exactly what it is. Press Enter.

If nothing has changed or something went wrong, restart your computer and read the menu list for details. It is possible that not only the Linux installation, but also various programs are present on the recorded image.

Then you should Install it from a Linux flash drive.

All the torment behind! Already at the beginning of the installation, you will be greeted by a friendly

Russian-language interface. Start by choosing a language. Select your preferred language.

Next, you need to make sure that the computer has enough free hard disk space, is connected to a power source, and is connected to the Internet. You can immediately agree that the latest updates are automatically downloaded during installation.

Click "Next." We get into the hard disk selection menu. In it, you can format and split partitions, if desired. Specify the partition (disk) in which you want to install the operating system and click the "Install Now" button.

We fall into the section change menu. Here you can increase the amount of memory, change the file system type, format the partition and specify the mount point. Use the "Ext4" file system and set the mount point "/". If there is no valuable information on the hard disk, it is advisable to format the partition. Click "Install Now".

Now we select the country and city of residence so that the system automatically sets the time and other indicators for your personal needs. Also, specify the keyboard layout. It remains to enter the desired name for your computer, a name for the user and a password (optional). Click "Next" and start the installation process.

After the installation is complete, restart the computer, remove the USB flash drive and wait for the Linux operating system to start.

How to make a bootable USB flash drive for Linux

Today, the operating system is becoming increasingly popular. Surely you have already heard from your friends or acquaintances stories about how easy it is to carry out such an installation. Obviously, creating a bootable USB flash drive for Linux is a great way to reinstall the operating system on a computer with a damaged or missing drive, laptop, or netbook. Let's get acquainted with this installation method better!

First, you need to find and download a Linux operating system image.

Finding images of different versions of Linux on the Internet is very simple because it is "freeware" and is distributed absolutely free. Download the desired image on our website, official website or torrents.

A bootable Linux flash drive requires a regular flash drive. Its volume should be 1GB and higher.

Next you need to download the program Unetbootin.

This program will help us with how to make a bootable Linux flash drive. You can download it from the page unetbootin.sourceforge.net. At the top of the site there are buttons for 3 distributions – Windows, Linux and Mac OS. If you, for example, now have Windows, then press the Windows button.

After downloading, the program opens instantly, and you do not need to install it. If you have problems with the launch (Windows 7), run "on behalf of the administrator."

Initially, the program is ticked on the "Distribution", but we need to put it on the "Disk Image". We also indicate that this is an ISO image. Next, click on the button "..." and select the image that we previously downloaded from the Internet.

If your flash drive is capacious enough, then it is advisable to allocate space in the file storage space. 100 MB will be enough.

And at the very bottom of the program window, select which flash drive you want to burn. Example –

"Type: USB drive; Media: E: \ ". If only one flash drive is inserted into the computer, the program will determine it on its own and there is no need to choose anything.

It remains only to press the "OK" button and wait until the program completes the burning of the image. It takes 5-10 minutes.

That is all you need to know about how to burn Linux to a USB flash drive. After burning, you must restart the computer or insert the USB flash drive into the computer where you want to install the Linux Operating System.

How to choose programs to install

So, the most crucial moment – the layout of the hard drive – is behind. Now the installation program proceeds to the next stage, in which it will offer to select the necessary programs (packages are traditionally called programs in Linux, which, by the way, is truer in terms of terminology).

You can simply choose one of the options for installing packages (for home computer, office, workstation with a connection to a local network, etc.). Alternatively, by turning on the Package selection switch manually, go to the software package selection window.

All programs included in the distribution of Linux are divided in this window into several sections: system, graphic, text, publishing, sound, games, documentation, and so on. In each section, you can select (or, conversely, deselect) any software package. If it is not clear from the name of the program what it is for, click on the name, and a brief description of the purpose of this program will appear in a special window. Unfortunately, in Russian-language distributions, often not all descriptions are translated into Russian, so some descriptions may be in English.

Having chosen the necessary packages for installation, be sure to locate on the screen and check the box to check dependencies. The fact is that some programs may depend on others, that is, they may use modules of other programs in their work.

Some programs may require the presence of any other software packages for normal operation. In this case, they say that one program depends on another. For example, the kreatecd CD burning program contains only a graphical user interface and calls the cdrecord console program for the actual recording, although the user doesn't see it when working.

This means that the kreatecd program depends on cdrecord. When installing Linux, all software dependencies are checked automatically; you just need to allow the installation program to do this by turning on the appropriate switch.

The checkbox for checking dependencies is needed for the installer to automatically check if some of the selected programs are using those packages that are not selected for installation. Having made such a check, the installation program will provide you with a list of these packages and will offer to install them as well. We should agree with this, otherwise, some programs will not work.

Configure devices and graphical interface

After you agree to install the necessary packages, the process of copying the necessary files to the hard disk will begin. This process is quite long, so you can go and drink coffee at this time, for at least five to ten minutes. However, if your distribution is recorded on two or more compact discs, the installer will from time to time ask you to insert the necessary compact disc into the drive.

Then the configuration of additional devices and the graphical interface will begin. There is one subtlety. The fact is that most installation programs for some reason incorrectly process information about the mouse. Therefore, the question of what kind of mouse you have at this stage is to answer a simple two-button or a simple three-button. Do not look in the list of the manufacturer, model, and so on.

After installing the system, it will be possible to separately enable additional functions of the mouse (for example, the operation of the scroll wheel) if they do not work themselves.

Install the bootloader

After all the above operations, the freshly installed system is ready for operation. However, the installer will ask you to answer one more question: should the boot loader be installed and, in most cases, if necessary, which one?

If Linux is the only operating system on your computer, then you will not need a bootloader. In this case, simply restart the computer, removing the bootable CD from it.

If you specifically changed the BIOS settings in order to allow the computer to boot from a CD or from a floppy disk, then now, after installing the system, you can reconfigure the computer to boot only from the hard disk. To do this, go back to the BIOS settings and change the boot order. However, if you specified the "universal" boot order – Floppy, CDROM, IDEO – you can no longer change it, just make sure that when you turn on and restart your computer, no boot diskettes or a CD are inserted in it, unless necessary boot from these devices.

Choosing the Right Linux Distributor

The popularity of the distribution. The more popular your distribution is, the easier it will be to find tutorials on it on the web. A large community means that you can easily get help in the forums dedicated to the distribution if you have any difficulties with its development. Finally, the more common the distribution, the more applications and packages are created for it. It is better to choose popular solutions with a ready base of packages than to suffer from the build from source in some exotic distribution.

The development command that deals with them. Naturally, it is better to pay attention to distributions supported by large companies like Canonical Ltd., Red Hat or SUSE, or to distributions with large communities.

Keep in mind that even the best Linux distributions have analogs that are not inferior to them.

Linux Mint

New users migrating from Windows definitely need to install Linux Mint. Today it is the most popular Linux distribution. This is a very stable and easy to use the system based on Ubuntu.

Linux Mint is equipped with a light and intuitive interface and a convenient application manager, so you will not have problems finding and installing programs. There are two shells: Cinnamon for modern computers and MATE for old computers. This is a very simple software that is suitable for ordinary users. You do not need any specific knowledge to install and use Mint.

There are of course disadvantages of this software. This is a large number of pre-installed programs that may never come in handy.

Manjaro

This is one of the newest Linux Distributors.

It is a popular Linux Distributor based on Arch. Arch is an incredibly powerful and functional distribution, but its KISS (Keep It Simple, Stupid) philosophy, as opposed to its name, makes it too complicated for beginners. Arch is installed only via the command line.

It, unlike Arch, has a simple graphical installer and at the same time combines the powerful features of Arch, such as AUR (Arch User Repository) and a sliding release. AUR is the richest source of Linux packages. If some application is in Linux, it probably already exists in AUR. So, in this distributor, you will always enjoy the freshest packages.

It comes with a variety of desktop shells to choose from: functional KDE, GNOME for tablet screens, Xfce, LXDE, and others. By installing this distributor, you can be sure that you get the latest updates first. This version has its own advantages of AUR, thanks to which you can install any application without unnecessary movements. Always fresh software. But, in truth, it has a peculiar design of the desktop shells. However, nothing prevents you from replacing it.

Debian

This distributor will take root well on your home server. It is a stable and conservative distribution that has become the basis for Ubuntu and many other Linux systems. It uses only the most trusted packages, making it a good choice for the server. It has stability and a large set of applications. But you will have to manually configure the distribution after installation.

Kodi

This is a Linux distribution, which is suitable for a media center. If you want to build your media server, choose this distributor. Strictly speaking, it is not a distribution kit, but a full-featured media player. You can install it in any Linux, but it is best to choose a bunch of Ubuntu + Kodi.

This distributor supports all types of video and audio files. It knows how to play movies, music, organize your photos. It will turn any connected TV into a universal entertainment device.

Thanks to the extensions, it can download media files through torrents, track the appearance of new seasons of your favorite TV shows, show videos from

YouTube and other streaming services. In short, Kodi can do everything.

In addition, Kodi is very beautiful and optimized for control from a remote control or device on Android. You can easily customize the Kodi interface using a variety of visual skins. It is very convenient to manage and has many functions.

But the standard interface of this may not appeal to everyone, but it is easy to replace.

There are also interesting versions: Linux distribution for desktop PC, this is Kubuntu;

A Linux distribution for an old personal computer, this is Lubuntu; The Linux version for the tablet or transformer is Ubuntu; The Linux version for the laptop is elementary OS and others.

Chapter 2. Linux installation

Before proceeding with the installation, it will be a good idea to check your PC's hardware first. You may check the hardware vendor's site to check the compatibility list.

DVD Drive: To install Linux, you must have a DVD drive, and your computer must be able to boot from the drive. If your hard drive controller is IDE/ATA or USB DVD, this will work in Linux.

Hard Drives: This is not necessary if you will be using the Live CD. If you will be installing Linux, it is ideal to have at least 4GB of disk space. Linux supports IDE and SCSI hard drive controllers.

Keyboard: All keyboards work with Linux.

Monitor: Most distribution installers can detect modern monitors. If you find that it does not display well, choose a monitor type and a specific resolution (1024x768).

Mouse: PS/2 or USB mouse works with Linux.

Network Card: Installers can detect most network cards. If you find that you are having problems with one, find additional information online.

Processor: Minimum processor speed required is 700 MHz New processor speeds nowadays are way more than this value.   In terms of speed, the higher the number, the better.

RAM: The bigger RAM, the better. The minimum required is 512MB. Check the corresponding RAM for your specific distro – others might require a bigger RAM allocation.

Sound Card, Video Card, Printer: Make sure that these are compatible with Linux. Refer to the hardware vendor's site for more information.

Next, make space for Linux.

If you opt to install Linux without removing your current OS, note that your existing operating system uses the whole hard drive. This means that Linux and your current OS needs to share the hard drive so that the two operating systems can co-exist. You will need to partition and divide the hard drive. If you choose to take this route, make sure to take a backup of your system because there is a risk of wiping out the data on the drive.

To facilitate partitioning, you can get hard drive partitioning products that run on Windows, or you can use a GUI called QTParted that comes with most Linux distributions. Some distributions (like openSUSE or Xandros Desktop) can reduce Windows partition and automatically create partitions for Linux. In case your distribution of choice offers this feature, you will no longer need a partitioning tool.

Installation Steps

Go to the Linux distribution site and download the distro file. The file that you downloaded will come with the installation steps. In this section, let's talk about the general installation steps for any Linux distribution.

Step 1: Prepare your CD/DVD installer or Live CD. Download a copy of the distribution you plan to install and burn it onto a CD/DVD.

Step 2: Ensure that your PC can boot from CD/DVD drive. If your PC still boots from the hard drive when you have a CD/DVD in the drive, change your Boot Devices first. Go into BIOS and change the order of boot devices – choose CD/DVD drive as the first boot option.

You can do this by rebooting your PC and pressing a key (F2 or Del on most computers) to go into the Setup menu. Verify the key for your computer brand and model. Once you assign CD/DVD drive as the first boot option, put the disk in the drive and reboot your computer.

Step 3: If you are using a Live CD, reboot your computer. The computer will then boot up and load the OS from your Live CD.

Once the installation is done, reboot your computer.

X is not working after installation

If you happen to see the GUI during the installation, but after the first reboot you are confronted with a grey screen or a black screen with an X in the middle, here are some steps that you can use to troubleshoot.

Reboot the PC. Press Ctrl+Alt+Delete.

Once the PC is booting up, press the A key if the distribution uses GRUB (GR and Unified Bootloader). For LILO, skip this step. The GRUB boot loader will then display a command line for the Linux kernel and will ask you to add what you want.

For GRUB, type a space and then word single. Press Enter. If using LILO, type Linux single then press Enter. The Linux kernel will boot in a single-user mode with the following prompt:

sh-3.00#

Once you see this prompt, you can now start to configure X.

Depending on the distribution you are using, X uses a configuration file to setup your display card, monitor, and resolution. The problem sometimes happens when the X configuration from the Linux installer is not right.

Solve this problem by creating a working configuration file:

Type the following command:

```
X -configure
```

Once you enter this command, the X server will create a configuration file. You'll see the screen go blank and then display several messages.

Use vi, a text editor and edit the file///etc./xorg.conf.new. Insert the linebelow afterSection "Files":line

```
FontPath "unix/:7100"
```

Start the X font server by typing the command below:

```
xfs
```

Type the line below to start the new configuration file.

```
X -config ///etc/xorg.conf.new
```

Once   you see the blank screen with an X cursor, the configuration file is working fine.

Use Ctrl+Alt+Backspace to stop the X server

Type the command below to copy the config file to the /etc/X11 directory:

```
cp ///etc/xorg.conf.new
```

Type the wordreboot or press Ctrl+Alt+Delete to reboot the computer.

The login screen should come up if the config file change went well.

Most, if not all, Linux distributions have a solid community online. If you encounter problems during the installation, search for the problem, describe it in detail, or use the actual error message as your search keyword. You will find the information that you need and if not, you can always post in the forums and the community will be ready to help.

Visit the following forums for more information:

Ubuntu: http://ubuntuforums.org/

Linux Mint: http://linuxmint.com/forum/

SUSE: https://forums.suse.com/forum.php

Debian: http://www.debianhelp.org/

Post-Installation Activities

Managing Hardware and Peripherals

CPU

The operating system keeps programs and hardware working together smoothly. The capabilities of Linux are affected by the limitations of your system's hardware (for example, disk space and memory) so it is important to know more details about your computer's hardware.

Let's start with the CPU. The CPU performs all the computing and its speed (in MHz) signifies how fast your computer can handle transactions. Your CPU specs will also tell you about the CPU family (most common are x86 and x86-64) and the number of cores that it has. To know more about your CPU, use the Linux commands below:

Hard Disk

Next, let's discuss your computer's hard disk. In the installation chapter, I spoke about the importance of making sure that your computer has enough disk space for Linux and the possible need for partitioning your hard disk if you want to run two operating systems at the same time.

If you plan on adding a new disk in the future, learning how to partition will come in handy. Linux supports the following partitioning tools:

Fdisk Tools – This is composed of the text-based tools: **fdisk**, **cfdisk,** and **sfdisk**. These tools are great for use in partitioning. However, it could be a bit overwhelming for beginners who are not yet familiar with partitioning.

libparted Tools – The **libparted** library presents both GUI and text-based partitioning tools. One particular example is GParted as shown in the screenshot below. The interface makes it easier to use for beginners.

GPT fdisk Tools – These are tools created for GPT (Globally Unique Identifier Partition Table) disks using the **fdisk** tools.

Here are some commands that you can use to check the existing disk space on your computer:

Removable Storage

Using storage such as USB flash drives and external hard disks in Linux works similarly when using Windows or Mac OS. Plug the device in and Linux will detect the device. Aside from accessing the drive via the desktop GUI, you can also navigate to the **/media** directory and find the mounted subdirectory.

After you use the removable media, unmount the disk before removing it to avoid any disk issues. You can generally right-click on the Device Name and click on any of the options such as **Unmount**, **Eject Volume**, or **Safely Remove**.

USB Devices

You can connect other devices such as human-interface devices (keyboard, mouse), cameras, mobile phones, scanners and printers to your Linux computer and expect that these work in a plug-and-play manner.

For printers, you will also need to set up the printer configuration after Linux detects the device. Follow the steps below to set-up a new printer. Note that the screenshots are taken from an Ubuntu distribution, but this is similar to the majority of the distros.

Click on **System Settings,** then **Printers** in the desktop. Provide the root password.

Click on the **Add** button. If the system detects your printer, the device will show in the list. Otherwise, you will need to continue with the configuration and provide the printer drivers. Click **Forward**.

Choose the correct driver. A list of available drivers will be shown – choose the one that is applicable for your printer make. If you do not find the driver on the list, you can also provide the printer driver or download the file online.

Fill-up the printer name and description.

Lastly, print a test page to make sure it's working.

Installing Additional Software

Linux-compatible softwares come in **.rpm** for RPM (Fedore, SUSE) or **.deb** for Debian (Debian, Ubuntu, Xandros) packages. Even if the type of packages varies, both RPM and Debian packages can be installed in any type of Linux distribution. Popularly used distributions provide a GUI for installing additional applications. In this section, I will discuss the ways of installing software in Ubuntu and Fedora.

Installing Applications in Ubuntu

Debian-based distros use APT or the Advanced Packaging Tool.

You can use the command below to install packages to your computer.

```
apt-get install package-name
```

This command will download the specific package name that you want to install. In case you do not know the package name, you can search for a keyword.

```
apt-cache search keyword
```

For example, I am looking for an application that I can use to take screenshots on (in) my GNOME desktop. I can further refine my search functionality with the following command:

```
apt-cache search screenshot | grep GNOME
```

The command will display the applicable lines that fit the search string:

```
shutter - feature-rich screenshot program
```

Shutter is the package name. Use the package name and run the **apt-get install** command again.

Aside from installing packages via the command line, you can also use the Software & Updates Tool. The GUI provides a simple and easy way to update your Ubuntu software and download packages.

Similar to Windows and Mac OS application stores, Ubuntu also has its Software Center where you can get new software and download the latest updates.

Installing Applications in Fedora

Fedora uses RPM packages. If you are using a GNOME desktop, you can simply use the Add or Remove Software tool (similar to Windows) to install new software.

Click on System⇨ Administration then on Add/Remove Software to access the menu. The utility will then display the Package Manager box showing the list of all packages. Select the corresponding check box and click on **Apply** or **Update** (if you are updating the packages). Clicking on the **Apply** button will install (or uninstall) the specific packages.

Chapter 3. Linux application

All Linux distros come with a robust selection of applications that you can use for almost all of your daily computing needs. Almost all of these applications are easily accessible using your distro's GUI desktop.

In this chapter, you will get to know some of the most common Linux applications and learn how to access them whenever you want to. You will also get to know some of the file managers used by different GUIs, which will allow you to make changes or browse files in your computer.

Where to Get Apps?

Almost all applications used by Linux have dedicated websites in which you can find detailed information about them, including details on where and how to download them. At the same time, all distros come with different sets of utilities and apps that you can choose to install as you setup your chosen distro.

If you have a missing app in a Debian or Debian-based distro, such as Ubuntu, you can easily get that application as long as you have a high-speed internet connection. For example, if you want to find out if there is a K3b CD/DVD burner available for a Debian

OS, simply key in the command apt-cache search
k3b. Doing so will return a result that looks like this:

```
k3b - A sophisticated KDE cd burning application
k3b-i18n - Internationalized (i18n) files for k3b
k3blibs - The KDE cd burning application library - runtime files
k3blibs-dev - The KDE cd burning application library - development files
```

If yu want to get this app, all you need to do is to
key in apt-get install k3b.

Office Tools and Applications

Average user or not, you will definitely need a
calculator, presentation applications, word processor,
calendars, and other staple office applications. There
is an abundance of these apps available for each
distro, which means that you can try them out to see
which ones will suit your needs better. While these
Linux apps may seem to be a little different than the
apps that you are used to, you will find that you will
get used to their interfaces after some sessions.

Here are some of the most commonly used office
applications that are available to Linux users:

- **LibreOffice Suite**

If you are used to using Microsoft Office for all your
office application needs, you will find that this suite
offers almost the same features. LibreOffice comes
with Calc spreadsheet application, the Impress app

which functions like Powerpoint, and the Writer app, which functions like Microsoft Word.

- **Kontakt**

This app comes with the KDE, which is integrated with other applications such as the KOrganizer, and the KMail. This application displays everything that you may want to pull up when you enter your desktop, such as your schedule, new emails, and more. All these information are summed up in a personal information manager that is available in a graphical format.

You can pull up Kontact by simply clicking on your desktop's panel icons or by launching it from the main menu. You can also explore all the apps that are integrated to Kontact by clicking on the icons located on the Kontact window's left pane.

- **Calculators**

You get a default calculator available to be used whether you are using GNOME or KDE. Both calculators are able to do scientific functions, such as trigonometry equations and getting square roots and inverses. To look for the calculator, pull up Accessories or Utilities from the main menu.

Using Multimedia Apps

Almost all Linux distros come with multimedia apps, which are mostly audio players and CD players. There are also some apps that are included that will allow you to use digital cameras or burn DVDs and CDs. If you want to play a video or a music file, you may need to download and install additional software.

Using Digital Cameras with Linux

Most of the distros available have a default application that you can use to import image files from digital cameras. Xandros and SUSE, for example, arrive with the digiKam app, which allows you to simply connect your digicam through the USB port and then import your image files from there.

digiKam functions like a typical file manager for media devices. To use it, follow these instructions:

1. **Attach your camera to the USB port or serial port, and then turn the camera on.**

2. Load digiKam. You can find the app under the Images or Graphics submenu. If you are loading the app for the first time, digiKam will ask you for the default location

where it will store image files, plus other preferences that you may want to configure.

3. Pull up the digiKam menu, and then go to Settings->Configure digiKam.

4. Select the Cameras tab, and then choose Auto Detect. If your camera is detected and supported but the app, then you can proceed using digiKam to download your photos from your device. You will see a new window that will display all your photos.

5. **Select the images that you want to save on your computer. After doing so, you can save the files in your target folder and even edit your photos with your chosen photo editor.**

If digiKam cannot find your digital camera, you can still access your files using the camera storage, as long as it comes with a USB interface. All you need to do is to follow the following steps:

1. **Connect the camera through the USB port**

Once the device is connected and detected, you can open the folder that contains your image files using the file manager window.

2. Select the photos that you want to save to your folder by dragging and dropping the files.

3. Close the file manager and eject the device.

How to Play Audio from a CD

All Linux distros come with default CD player apps. If you want to play music from a CD, all you need to have is a Linux-configured sound card.

In some distros, a dialog box will pop up to ask you whether you want to play the CD that you inserted in the drive or not. If you do not see this dialog box, you can find your CD player by selecting Applications->Sound and Video.

If you are using the KDE CD player, you will see the name of the CD and the current track being played. This player retrieves the album information from freedb.org, which is an Internet-based open source database for CDs. To download the album information, you will need to be connected to the internet. However, once you are able to download this information, your computer caches the data which can be used for future sessions.

How to Play Sound Files

If you want to play any sound file, such as .mp3s, you can use either the XMMS or the Rhythmbox. Rhythmbox is one of the preferred players by users that has large .mp3 collections because it can be useful when it comes to organizing their files. You can pull up Rhythmbox by locating it from the main menu.

When you use Rhythmbox for the first time, an app assistant will prompt you to identify where your music files are stored. Doing so will allow the application to manage your music library. Afterwards, Rhythmbox will display your songs in an orderly manner.

XMMS is another option that you may have, especially if you have a music library that contains several file types, such as FLAC, .wav, or Ogg Vorbis. To run this application, simply select the app icon from the main menu. When you start XMMS, you can select a file by choosing Window-> Play File, or by hitting the L key. On the dialog box Load File, select one or multiple files that you want to load. Upon clicking the Play button, the application will play the selected file/s.

How to Burn a Disc In Linux

Most of the Linux file managers available now are capable of burning a DVD or a CD Disc. For example, the Nautilus and the Xandros file managers have built-in capability for burning discs. At the same time, different Linux distros also offer applications that will allow you to conveniently burn files into a DVD or CD. For example, the app K3b allows you to burn discs in distros such as SUSE and Knoppix.

Applications such as K3b are easy to use – all you need to do is to gather all the files that you want to burn into a disc and then start the burning process with the app. However, take note that these applications may need command line programs, such as cdrdao and cdrecord in order to burn CDs. K3b also requires the growisofs program to be able to burn DVDs.

Graphics and Imaging Apps

Linux also offers different imaging and graphics manipulation applications. Two of the most popular apps are the following:

The GIMP

The GIMP is a program that is released under the GNU GPL (General Public License). Most of the Linux distros come with this application, but you may also have to select a package in order to install this program. The GIMP is often compared to the most popular image-manipulation applications out there, such as Adobe Photoshop and PhotoPaint.

To launch The GIMP, pull up the main menu and then select the application in the Graphics category. Once you start the program, you will see a window that will show you the license and the copyright information. Proceed with the installation by clicking on the Continue button.

Tip: If you can't locate The GIMP, add the program by going to the Add/Remove Software (found in System Settings) and install the application from there.

Installing the GIMP will create a subdirectory in your home directory, which will hold all the data that you need in order to store preferences that you make to the application. Click the Continue button in order for the app to proceed creating these directories, and then follow the instructions detailed by the wizard to finish the installation. After the installation, The GIMP will then load plugins, or modules that are designed to enhance the app's functionality. Once all plugins are loaded, you can browse on tips that will be displayed on the Tip window.

GNOME Ghostview

This application is best for viewing PDF (.pdf)and PostScript (.ps) documents or printing these document files. Ghostview allows you to view and print selected pages found on a long document, as well as magnify or zoom out on document sections. You can find this application by going to Graphics->Post Script Viewer in Fedora.

Chapter 4. Becoming a Linux power user

In Linux, this command prompt offers a very powerful way for managing users. You can use the command line to create and delete users. These users can also be assigned certain privileges as to what they can or cannot do with the system and its files. This shows how the terminal is a powerful tool. These users can also be grouped together into a single group. Addition and deletion of these users from a group is also possible. This is what we are going to explore in this chapter.

'Group' Commands

In Linux, groups are defined in the file '/etc/group file'. This file contains the name of the group, its id and the list of users belonging to each particular group. To check the available groups in your system, run the following command:

    $ groups

```
ubuntu@ubuntu-desktop:~/Desktop$ groups
ubuntu adm dialout cdrom plugdev lpadmin admin sambashare
ubuntu@ubuntu-desktop:~/Desktop$
```

From the figure above, it is very clear that my system has 8 groups. If you need to create a new group and give it the name 'group1', run the following command:

groupadd group1

It is worth noting that most Linux distros create a group for the user and give it the name they have used as the account name. Once you have created your group using the above command, it is important to verify that it has really been created. This can be done by viewing the contents of the file '/etc/group'. If you can't find the name of the group, you have created then something must have gone wrong with its addition. The contents of this file can be viewed either in the command window or can be opened in the vim editor as follows:

cat /etc/group   -or-   vi /etc/group

However, if you use the second method, that is, viewing it on the vim editor, make sure that you don't alter its contents as this might result into errors. To add the group id to your group, use the '–g' option as shown below:

Groupadd –g 1300 group1id

To create a system group, use the –r option as shown below:

Groupadd –r systemgroup

We can now use the 'useradd' command which can be used for either a new user to the system or for updating the information of any available user. Let us create a new user named 'user1':

useradd -c "User" -d "/home/user1" -s "/bin/bash" –user1

In the above command, we have used many parameters. Let us define their purpose:

1. '-c' - this will be used to designate the name of the user. It is the name to be displayed on the login window. In our case, this is "User".
2. '-d' - the path signifying the user's home directory. If you don't specify this, it will be created by default. In our command above '/home/user1' will be our user's home directory.
3. '-s' - this will establish the default login shell for the user we have created. In our case the default shell for 'user1' will be the 'bash' shell.

Other options that can be used together with the 'useradd' command include the following:

4. '-b' - specifies the base directory of the system. This is the '/home' for most Linux distros and is used for the purpose of the home directory. If we don't specify the '-d' option above while creating a new user, this is made the default home directory for the new user.

5. '-g' - this specifies the primary group name or ID. If you don't specify this option while creating a new user, a new group with a name similar to the login name is created and a group id is assigned.

Example:

useradd –g 200 user1

6. '-G' - this specifies other supplementary groups which the user is also a member of. A comma is used to separate the group names.
Example:

71

useradd −g 200 −G sudo, adm user1

Note that in the above command, we have specified only two groups. Others can also be added and a comma is used to separate them as well.

Now that we have created a new user and assigned them a group, it is important to assign them a password. This will ensure security and that no other user will login to the system and act as them. To assign a password for the user we have created above, that is, user1, run the following command:

passwd user1

Once you run this command, you will be prompted the password and also to retype the same password. The user user1 will then use that password to login to the system. The passwd command is also associated with other options which include the following:

1. '-d' - this deletes the password associated with the specified user, meaning that this user will not be able to login to the system anymore. **Example:**

passwd –d user1

2. '-S' – this shows all the information in the '/etc/shadow' file so as to show the user's status.
Example:

passwd –S user1

3. '-l' - this locks the password for a particular user's account. The user will then be able to login to the system without authentication. Other means of authentication such as SSH (secure shell) will then be used for authentication purposes.

4. -a- used to show the status of all the users of the system. It can only be combined with the –S option.

Example:

passwd –S –a

Sometimes, you might need to modify some of the settings for a certain user. This is easy to do via the command line as explained below.

useradd -c "User" -d "/home/user1" -s "/bin/bash" –user1

To change both the login and the name of the above user as well as the ID, or to add him to the group admin use the following command:

usermod -l user -c "The User" -u 4000 -G adm -a user1

The –l option has the purpose of creating a new login name for the user. To delete a group, use the 'groupdel' command as shown below:

groupdel group1

The group will be deleted, however, this will only happen if the group is a supplementary group for the users. If it is the primary group, then we need to start by first deleting the users before deleting the group.

To delete a certain user, just run the following command:

userdel user1

The above command will delete the user 'user1' from the system. However, if he is logged into the system at this time, you will be warned before deleting. The files and the home directory for this user will not be deleted. The 'userdel' command is also associated with the following options:

1. **'-r' - all the directories and files in the home directory of the user will also be removed.**
   Example:

   Userdel –r user1

2. '-f' - this option will force the account of the user to be deleted regardless of whether or not they are logged into the system. The home directory of this user will also be removed regardless of whether other users are using this directory or not.

Example:

userdel –f user1

For a user to be able to execute this command, they must be added to the sudo group which is a system group. To add a user to this group, simply run the following command:

usermod -G sudo -a user1

In the above command, we have added the user 'user1' to the system group 'sudo'. This user will then be able to use the 'sudo' command. For the user to be in full administrative control of their account, they must be added the 'adm' group. This can be done as follows:

usermod -G sudo,adm -a user1

If the user wants to login to the system via the shell, the following command should be used:

login user1

They will then be prompted to enter the password and if correct, they will be able to access the system. To checks the groups of a certain user, execute the following command:

groups 'username'

Example:

groups user1

The above command will show all the groups to which the user 'user1' belongs.

Chapter 5. Using the Shell

Effective Linux professional is unthinkable without using the command line.

The command line is a shell prompt that indicates the system is ready to accept a user command. This can be called a user dialogue with the system. For each command entered, the user receives a response from the system:

1. another invitation, indicating that the command is executed, and you can enter the next.

2. error message, which is a statement of the system about events in it, addressed to the user.

Users who are accustomed to working in systems with a graphical interface, working with the command line may seem inconvenient. However, in Linux, this type of interface has always been basic, and therefore well developed. In the command shells used in Linux, there are plenty of ways to save effort, that is, keystrokes when performing the most common actions:

automatic addition of long command names or file names

searching and re-executing a command that was once performed before

substitution of file name lists by some pattern, and much more

The advantages of the command line are especially obvious when you need to perform similar operations on a variety of objects. In a system with a graphical interface, you need as many mice dragging as there are objects, one command will be enough on the command line.

This section will describe the main tools that allow you to solve any user tasks using the command line: from trivial operations with files and directories, for example, copying, renaming, searching, to complex tasks requiring massive similar operations that occur as in the user's application work, when working with large data arrays or text, and in system administration.

Shells

A command shell or command interpreter is a program whose task is to transfer your commands to the operating system and application programs, and their answers to you. According to its tasks, it corresponds to command.com in MS-DOS or cmd.exe in Windows, but functionally the shell in Linux is incomparably richer. In the command shell language, you can write small programs to perform a series of sequential operations with files and the data they contain — scripts.

Having registered in the system by entering a username and password, you will see a command line prompt – a line ending in $. Later this symbol will be used to denote the command line. If during the installation a graphical user interface was configured to start at system boot, then you can get to the command line on any virtual text console. You need to press Ctrl-Alt-F1 - Ctrl-Alt-F6 or using any terminal emulation program, for example, xterm.

The following shells are available. They may differ depending on the distributor:

bash

The most common shell for Linux. It can complement the names of commands and files, keeps a history of commands and provides the ability to edit them.

pdkdh

The korn shell clone, well known on UNIX shell systems.

sash

The peculiarity of this shell is that it does not depend on any shared libraries and includes simplified implementations of some of the most important utilities, such as al, dd, and gzip. Therefore, the sash is especially useful when recovering from system crashes or when upgrading the version of the most important shared libraries.

tcsh

Improved version of C shell.

zsh

The newest of the shells listed here. It implements advanced features for autocompletion of command arguments and many other functions that make working with the shell even more convenient and efficient. However, note that all zsh extensions are disabled by default, so before you start using this command shell, you need to read its documentation and enable the features that you need.

The default shell is bash Bourne Again Shell. To check which shell you're using, type the command: echo $ SHELL.

Shells differ from each other, not only in capabilities but also in command syntax. If you are a novice user, we recommend that you use bash, further examples describe the work in this particular area.

Bash shell

The command line in bash is composed of the name of the command, followed by keys (options), instructions that modify the behavior of the command. Keys begin with the character – or –, and often consist of a single letter. In addition to keys, after the command, arguments (parameters) can follow – the names of the objects on which the command must be executed (often the names of files and directories).

Entering a command is completed by pressing the Enter key, after which the command is transferred to the shell for execution. As a result of the command execution on the user's terminal, there may appear messages about the command execution or errors, and the appearance of the next command line prompt (ending with the $ character) indicates that the command has completed, and you can enter the next one.

There are several techniques in bash that make it easier to type and edit the command line. For example, using the keyboard, you can:

Ctrl-A

go to the beginning of the line. The same can be done by pressing the Home key;

Ctrl-u

delete current line;

Ctrl-C

Abort the execution of the current command.

You can use the symbol; in order to enter several commands in one line. bash records the history of all commands executed, so it's easy to repeat or edit one of the previous commands. To do this, simply select the desired command from the history: the up key displays the previous command, the down one and the next one. In order to find a specific command among those already executed, without flipping through the whole story, type Ctrl-R and enter some keyword used in the command you are looking for.

Commands that appear in history are numbered. To run a specific command, type:

! command number

If you enter !!, the last command typed starts.

Sometimes on Linux, the names of programs and commands are too long. Fortunately, bash itself can complete the names. By pressing the Tab key, you can complete the name of a command, program, or directory. For example, suppose you want to use the bunzip2 decompression program. To do this, type:

bu

Then press Tab. If nothing happens, then there are several possible options for completing the command. Pressing the Tab key again will give you a list of names starting with bu. For example, the system has buildhash, builtin, bunzip2 programs:

```
$ bu

buildhash builtin bunzip2

$ bu
```

Type n> (bunzip is the only name whose third letter is n), and then press Tab. The shell will complete the name and it remains only to press Enter to run the command!

Note that the program invoked from the command line is searched by bash in directories defined in the PATH system variable. By default, this directory listing does not include the current directory, indicated by ./ (dot slash). Therefore, to run the prog program from the current directory, you must issue the command ./prog.

Basic commands

The first tasks that have to be solved in any system are: working with data (usually stored in files) and managing programs (processes) running on the system. Below are the commands that allow you to perform the most important operations on working with files and processes. Only the first of these, cd, is part of the actual shell, the rest are distributed separately, but are always available on any Linux system. All the commands below can be run both in the text console and in graphical mode (xterm, KDE console). For more information on each command, use the man command, for example:

man ls

cd

Allows you to change the current directory (navigate through the file system). It works with both absolute and relative paths. Suppose you are in your home directory and want to go to its tmp / subdirectory. To do this, enter the relative path:

cd tmp /

To change to the / usr / bin directory, type (absolute path):

cd / usr / bin /

Some options for using the command are:

cd ..

Allows you to make the current parent directory (note the space between cd and ..).

cd -

Allows you to return to the previous directory. The cd command with no parameters returns the shell to the home directory.

ls

ls (list) lists the files in the current directory. Two main options: -a - view all files, including hidden, -l - display more detailed information.

rm

This command is used to delete files. Warning: deleting the file, you cannot restore it! Syntax: rm filename.

This program has several parameters. The most frequently used ones are: -i - file deletion request, -r - recursive deletion (i.e. deletion, including subdirectories and hidden files). Example:

rm -i ~ / html / *. html

Removes all .html files in your html directory.

mkdir, rmdir

The mkdir command allows you to create a directory, while rmdir deletes a directory, provided it is empty. Syntax:

mkdir dir_name

rmdir dir_name

The rmdir command is often replaced by the rm -rf command, which allows you to delete directories, even if they are not empty [26].

less

less allows you to page by page. Syntax:

less filename

It is useful to review a file before editing it; The main use of this command is the final link in a chain of programs that outputs a significant amount of text that does not fit on one screen and otherwise flashes too quickly [27]. To exit less, press q (quit).

grep

This command allows you to find a string of characters in the file. Please note that grep searches by a regular expression, that is, it provides the ability to specify a template for searching a whole class of words at once. In the language of regular expressions, it is possible to make patterns describing, for example, the following classes of strings: "four digits in a row, surrounded by spaces". Obviously, such an expression can be used to search in the text of all the years written in numbers. The search capabilities for regular expressions are very wide. For more information, you can refer to the on-screen documentation on grep (man grep). Syntax:

grep search_file

ps

Displays a list of current processes. The command column indicates the process name, the PID (process identifier) is the process number (used for operations with the process — for example, sending signals with the kill command). Syntax:

ps arguments

Argument u gives you more information, ax allows you to view those processes that do not belong to you.

kill

If the program stops responding or hangs, use this command to complete it. Syntax:

kill PID_number

The PID_number here is the process identification number, You can find out the process number for each executable program using the ps command. Normally, the kill command sends a normal completion signal to the process, but sometimes it does not work, and you will need to use kill -9 PID_number. In this case, the command will be immediately terminated by the system without the possibility of saving data (abnormal). The list of signals that the kill command can send to a process can be obtained by issuing the command kill -l.

Chapter 6. How to use Linux desktop

Now that you have Linux running on your computer, you will want to learn the basics. If you are coming from Windows or Mac OS, things will look different, but don't become discouraged. You have already learned how to install new software, so make sure that you find everything you need. Once you are happy with your selection of software, let's start to explore the rest of Linux.

When you have logged in, you will be shown the desktop, much like with Windows and Mac OS. This is your primary working area. In Ubuntu 10.10, there will be a panel across the top, as well as one on the bottom of the screen. Just like with other graphical operating systems, you will move the cursor around with your mouse, and click on icons to activate them. See, it's not that different, is it?

Desktop Panels

The bars on the top and bottom of the screen are panels, but you can customize your panels in a huge number of ways. By doing this, you can essentially create the Linux experience that perfectly suits your needs. For many, this is not needed, so don't feel obliged to experiment with your panels. If you like the default experience, that is all you need to use.

Your panels provide a place for you to start, when interacting with the desktop environment. They also give you various pieces of information about your computer. Notifications will appear on your panels as well. If you like, you can place your panels on the sides of the screen, by accessing the properties of your system.

Accessibility Options

If you need special accessibility options, like larger icons, or an on-screen keyboard, there will be an icon to access these. It is different for various systems; it looks like an illustration of a person inside a circle for some. Clicking on this icon will take you to a list of options, such as turning on a screen reader, magnifying glass, changing the colors in contrast, sticky keys, ignoring duplicate key presses, and pressing and holding keys.

Navigation

In order to move around inside your system, and access various files and software, you will need to learn how to navigate Linux. This sounds more difficult than it actually is. While different versions of Linux vary in how they deal with navigation, the process is pretty easy to pick up. If you click on your system settings, you will be taken to a list of options. Clicking on an option will take you to more options, etc., until you arrive where you want to go. The main menus are like tables of contents, and they will show you the more detailed sections of each part of your computer system.

If you are used to using Windows or Mac OS, it should not take you long to figure out how to navigate through your computer. If you cannot find something, simply perform a search, and type in what you want to find. Ubuntu is especially powerful in this respect, as you can access a system, and online, search by using the Windows key on your keyboard.

Command line is based on text, unlike the GUIs (graphical user interfaces) that people generally use these days. However, it can often be must simpler to use command line, especially when you want to get something done quickly. Do you remember the old days when Microsoft DOS was popular? You might recall seeing people working on computers, using nothing but text commands to get things done. That is what Linux command line does. There are different pieces of software for command line, and distributions will have their own versions. You can also install your own choice of command line application.

The very thought of using command line scares a lot of people, and they have no desire to do so. However, since you are reading this section, let's assume that you want to learn about command line, and begin with some basic commands. One great thing about working with command line is that you can work with a range of different Linux distributions, and always be able to do things the same way, with command line. Another reason that people like using command line is the pure power it gives them, although it is a little more complex to learn than graphical user interfaces.

Open up your command line software, which is also knows as your system's shell. This is called Terminal in Ubuntu, and you can find your shell with a quick system search. The keyboard shortcut to access Terminal is Ctrl + Alt + T, and this shortcut is the same for many versions of Linux.

Sudo

While learning to install software, you learned about the sudo command. You will need to enter this at the start of some commands, where admin privilege is required, but you should not use sudo for ordinary commands.

File and Directory Commands

In order to access different parts of your system, you will need to look at directories, and the files they contain. Directories are the folders of your system, containing files, and more folders with files, etc.

Here is a list of commands that will help you to navigate your files and directories:

- "~" indicates your home directory, such as /home or /home/user (with your username in the place of user).

- "ls" This will display a list of the files in the directory that you are currently looking at.

- "pwd" means "print working directory" and will tell you which directory you are currently in.

- "cd" will let you "change directory", so that you can move around to different parts of your system.

- If you type "cd /" you will be taken to your root, or base-level directory, so that's a good starting point if you become lost.

- "cd" and "cd ~" are two commands that will take you to your home directory.

- "cd .." Will go back up one directory.

- "cd -" will simply go back to the previous directory that you were in.

- You don't have to go through one directory at a time, if you know where you want to navigate. Let's say that you want to go to your "Documents" directory, which is located in a directory called "My Stuff". This might involve the command, "cd /my stuff/documents".

- If you want to copy a file, use "cp" by entering "cp file mine /directory" where "mine" is the name of the file that you wish to copy, and "directory" is where you want to copy the file to. You can copy a directory in the same way, with the command "cp -r directory mine" where "mine" is a directory instead of a file.

- If you want to move a file (as with cut & paste), use the "mv" command instead of "cp".

- To delete a file, use "rm" with the name of the file, where "rm" stands for remove.

- To delete an empty directory, use "rmdir".

- To delete a directory, as well as anything that is inside, including directories and files, use "rm -r"

- Create a new directory with the command "mkdir".

- "man" will show you a manual of commands. If you want a manual of the types of manuals, you can enter "man man".

Those are the basics of navigating files and directories with command line, as well as moving them around. In a graphical interface, these are similar to dragging, dropping, cutting, and pasting files and folders, as well as simply clicking into different folders.

Running Files

Now that you have an idea of how to move around in your system, using the command line, it's time to run some files. It's pretty simple, and you can do it with this command:

"./nameoffile.extension"

In this example, "nameoffile" is the name of the file that you want to run, while ".extension" is the extension of the file. If you wanted to run text document called "story", you would type "./story.txt", as ".txt" is the correct extension for text files.

Remember that you can "ls" (list) the files in a directory, to make sure that it contains the one that you want to run.

If this is becoming too complex for you to understand, don't worry. You can always go back to using the graphical interface when you become stuck and keep practicing with the command line in your own time.

System Commands

If you want to find out some information about your system, you can do that using command line as well. Here is a list of system information commands:

• To find out how much space has been used on your disks, use "df -h". There are other ways to do this, but the "h" here stands for "human readable", and it will display the information in megabytes.

•   Use the command "du" to find out how much space a particular directory is using. This will show you information for all files, and directories, inside a directory. If you would rather an overview of the space used, the command "du -sh" will do this (with "s" meaning "summary" and "h" once again meaning "human readable").

•   To look at the total amounts of both used and free memory on your computer system, use the "free" command. To see this in megabytes, use the command "free -m".

•   To see an overview of the processes that are running on your system, use the "top" command (which stands for "table of processes"). After you have finished looking at your table of processes, you will need to press "q" to exit.

•   To get an overview of all system information, use the command "uname -a".

•   If you want information about the Linux distribution that you are currently running, use the command "lsb_release -a".

- To see information about your networks, use the command "ip addr".

Adding New Users

You have already set up your own login details, but you can also add new users to your system. This is helpful if there will be more than one person using your computer.

To create a new user on your computer, use the following command:

- "adduser newuser", where "newuser" will be the user name of the person that you are adding. You can make this whatever you like.

- "passwd newuser" will let you give your new user a password.

Using Options

You can add options to your commands, and some of the commands listed have shown you how to do this. If you were to use the command "ls -s", that would use the "ls" command for listing the contents of a directory, with the "-s" option for adding file sizes as well. Another common option is the "-h" command, that you have already looked at, which makes the sizes "human readable".

If you were to type "ls -sh", you would be asking for a listing of the contents of a directory, and adding the options to show the sizes of everything, as well as displaying those sizes in megabytes, instead of blocks.

Keyboard Shortcuts

If you want to do something in Linux, and you use your graphical interface to look online for help, you will often find command line text that you can use. You don't need to understand anything about using these commands, and you can still benefit from them. You will need to copy the text, by highlighting it with your mouse in a normal fashion. However, if you try to use the common keyboard shortcut "Ctrl + V" to paste into the command line shell, it will not work. To paste text with command line, press "Ctrl + Shift + V" instead.

Using command line might seem like an awful lot of typing, but there are more keyboard shortcuts that you can use to save time:

102

- Down arrow (or Ctrl + N): go back to your previous command.

- Up arrow (or Ctrl + P): go through your previous commands.

- Enter: <u>enter</u> the command, once you have found what you are looking for, or you have typed what you want.

- Tab: will automatically complete file names and commands. If there is more than one option, it will give you a list to choose from.

- Ctrl + R: will let you search through the commands that you have already entered. This is extremely useful for when you have entered some long commands. Simply use this keyboard shortcut, and then type part of the command that you want. It will then display commands that start with the text you have entered. Press Enter when you have found what you are looking for.

- "History": entering this command will display a history of every command that you have used, next to a number. If there are too many commands to display, use the command "history | less" to give you a list that you can scroll through.

Use an Integrated Development Environment

We already explored the process of using the command line terminal to write and execute code for Linux in Python. There is another option for doing this, and that is to use an Integrated Development Environment, or IDLE (you might could say that IDLE is a play on the fact that programmers tend to be lazy and are constantly looking for shortcuts). Ubuntu can be downloaded with a graphics IDLE, or you can download one separately. IDLE is written in Python, which makes it much easier to implement the code that you write.

IDLE is a great program for beginner coders to use for several reasons. One is that it automatically colors different syntax features in different colors, making finding mistakes much easier. For example, key words, text, and comments will all appear in different colors. Just like highlighting in your college textbooks made finding what you need to study much easier, color-coding these different features makes finding your mistakes much easier.

Another reason is because it uses a graphical user interface (GUI) instead of a command line interface. This makes it much more user friendly and easy to navigate.

When using IDLE, you don't necessarily need a text editor. You can write your code directly into IDLE, then execute it. If you are new to coding, you may want to consider using IDLE before moving on to the command line terminal.

IDLE does have a number of problems associated with it, so many programmers prefer to move on from it to the command line terminal as soon as possible.

Write Patches

Keep in mind that there are many different methods to writing a patch. This is just one of them.

Diff is a command line program utilized by the Linux core development team. It compares the original source code with the changes that someone has proposed and shows exactly what needs to be done to implement those changes. You need to keep the original source code for the particular area that you want to improve, and also write out the source code for your patch. You don't need to download a particular program; it is usually pre-packed with Linux operating systems. If you find that there is a problem in the execution of your code, you can compare your patch to the original source code using Diff to try to figure out where the problem is.

There are a few challenges that present themselves when you want to get started with writing a patch. The first is that the source code for the Linux kernel is 15 **million** lines long. You would have to be incredibly dedicated and disciplined in order to sit down and read through all of it! The thought of that much code may be so overwhelming that you don't even know where to start. The good news is that there are multiple points of entry for you to more easily find a specific location. You just have to find the right one and consider that your starting place.

Additionally, another good place to get started with finding your way through the 15 million lines of source code is to look for the overall data structures. If you are trying to map your way through a forest, you don't start by looking at the minute characteristics of individual trees. Instead, you start by trying to imagine a bird's eye view of the entire forest. In other words, you try to understand the overall structure (the data structure), and then you can figure out a path through the structure (the bits and pieces of the source code).

Another problem associated with getting started with the source code so that you can write a patch is the language. The kernel is written in C, but it is much more complicated than a standard C program. Reading the source code requires an advanced understanding of the C programming language. If you are not familiar with it, you may want to partner with somebody who is.

Nevertheless, you can write a patch using Python. Obviously, the first thing you will need to do is isolate the segment of code that you want to modify. Maybe there are multiple changes that you want to make. Once you have isolated the code, you will need to write out your changes. Again, your changes may be written in Python, while the source code is in C. We'll solve that problem in the next step.

Cython is a compiler that translates between Python and C, as well as some other programming languages. You can use it to translate your patch code so that it can be applied to the source code.

Cython is also a programming language that allows for C-based extensions to Python; make sure that you download the compiler. Using the compiler to translate Python into C is probably the fastest and easiest way of getting the job done.

Once you have written in your patch, you want to test it out on your own computer. Run it in the command line terminal to see if it runs the way that you want it to run. The easiest way for your code to get rejected by the Linux core development team is for it to not work! Keep modifying it until it works exactly how you want it to work.

Implement it on your own computer. That's right. You can run the patched code on your own computer, even if it isn't part of the Linux kernel. If it makes your computer run more optimally, then it may be time to take some steps to share it with the world as an indie programmer.

Share it with friends. Do you know people who use Linux and might be interested in the patch that you made? Maybe you have some friends, programming cronies, or family members who are Linux enthusiasts (even if they are just getting started with

Linux) and would be thrilled to have your patch applied to their computers.

Share it on forums. GitHub and Stack Overflow are just two forums that are frequented by members of the Linux community. There are so many Linux users who use forums that, if you share your patch through them, you will likely find plenty of people who want to implement it on their own computers. You will need to upload it as a .tar file so that others can download it and execute it.

And who knows? Your patch may become so ubiquitous that it ends up being accepted by the core development team as a part of the kernel after all!

Chapter 7. Working with the Command Line

A command line is also referred to as a terminal. This is a text-based user interface to the system. With command line, the user can enter commands by simply typing them on the keyboard. When you run the command by pressing Enter on the keyboard, you get feedback as a text.

To break this content down:

Line 1: this presents the prompt to us as user bash. Once we have the prompt, we are supposed to enter a command, in this case, ls. This means that typically, a command is the first thing that we have to type. After which, we are supposed to key in an argument in the command line (-l/home/Gary). In this case, the first thing that you have to bear in mind is that these are separated by spaces. That is, after typing the command, then you put in space before you can type in the argument. The first argument that we have used in this case **−l** is also referred to as an option. Options play a significant role in modifying the behavior of a command. They are often listed before other arguments, and they begin with a dash (-)

Line 2-5: These represent the outputs that we get once we run the commands, we keyed in. Most of the commands that we key into the terminal will yield outputs that will be listed immediately after the command. However, there are other commands that when you run them, they will not display the results or any information unless in cases of error.

Line 6: This presents the prompt once again. Once you run the command that you typed into the terminal, and you have the results after running the command, you get a prompt. This means that if the prompt is not displayed after running a certain command, then this indicates that the command is still running. One important thing that I want you to know is that while on a terminal, you might not have the numberings on each line. This was just for me to explain what each line represents.

How then do we open a terminal?

When working with Linux, the first thing that you have to learn is to know how to open a terminal. It is fairly easy. It is kind of hard to tell you how to do it based on the fact that every system is different. However, some of the few places that you can begin are these:

If you are using Mac, the first thing you do is go to applications and then click on utilities. Under utilities, you have a terminal option which you select, and there you have a working terminal to type your commands. Alternatively, the best and easiest key combinations to opening a Linux terminal is "command + space." This combination will bring up a spotlight where you will type terminal and it will soon after showing up on the screen. You can also download MobaXterm and use it on Mac (http://macdownload.informer.com/macterm/downlo ad/) as a local terminal.

If you are working on Linux, then you will be able to access a terminal by clicking on systems and then applications. Under applications, you select utilities and select the terminal option. Alternatively, you can do this by simply right-clicking on a blank space on the desktop, and a drop-down menu will appear. Select the "open in terminal" option, and there you are!

If you are using Windows, there are some ways you can use a terminal. The best one is using an SSH client to access the Linux terminal where you can run your commands. Some examples of application software that will allow you to do this are MobaXterm (http://download.cnet.com/MobaXterm/3000-7240_4-10890137.html) and Putty (http://www.putty.org/). With this software, the first thing is to download them online and install them on your Pc. On the desktop, you will have the shortcut that you can click on every time you need the terminal.

In other words, it is the root account that often plays a significant role when the user is running privileged commands as well as while maintaining the system. Therefore, for you to create a user account, the first important step is to log in to the root and use the **useradd** or **adduser** command. When using the Windows MobaXterm or Putty application, you simply click on the shortcut on your desktop, and a window terminal will appear. Then you will be prompted to log in as follows:

user@bash: **ssh** Gary@hpc.ucdavis.edu.uk

Unauthorized access is prohibited.

ssh Gary@hpc.ucdavis.edu.uk's Password:

Last login: Fri Feb 17 14:34:27 2017 from 40.290.160.11

Once you enter the account username, the system will prompt you to key in a password for that account as shown above. When you are entering the password, the characters that you are typing will not be echoed to the screen. This means that you have to type very carefully. The main reason is that when you mistype the password, you will need a message log in incorrect, and this means that you have to try again. Once you have entered the password correctly for your account, then you are free to access the files and directories in that account.

The Shell, Bash

Within the terminal, there is a shell. This is part of the operating system that plays a significant role in defining the manner in which the terminal will behave. It also looks after execution of commands for you. There is a broad range of shells available, but the most common one is referred to as bash. This denotes "**Bourne again shell**." This Linux tutorial will make the assumption that you are using bash as your shell. However, if you wish to know what shell you are using, then the best thing to do is use the command echo. This command plays an important role in displaying a system variable that states the current shell in use. In other words, the command echo is used to display messages. As long as everything that it prints on the screen ends with the term bash, then you know that all is well.

user@bash: **echo $SHELL**

/bin/bash

user@bash:

Shortcuts

I have mentioned this before, but I will tell you again that the use of Linux terminal for running commands can be daunting at times, but the most important thing is that you should not fret. This is because Linux is full of shortcuts that will sure make your life super easy. I will introduce you to several of them throughout this tutorial, and by the time you are done, you will never leave Linux! The most important thing is for you to take note of them as we go along as they do not just make your life easy but will save you from making those silly mistakes such as typos.

One of the most important shortcuts is using the up and down arrow key on your keyboard. When you are typing commands on Linux, they are kept in a history. The simplest way you can traverse this history is using these two keys. This means that the commands that you have used before do not need any retyping. You simply hit the up arrow a few times to get the command that you are looking for. Additionally, to edit the commands that you have used before, you can use the left and right arrow keys to move the cursor to where you need to perform edits.

essential Linux commands

In this chapter we explain basic Linux commands that will help you to deal with files and directories, text processing commands, users and groups, process management, networks, and the help system.

7.1 Files and Directories

touch

The **touch** command is used to update the access date or modification date of a file and works in two ways: if the file already exists, the timestamp for access and modification of the file is set to the current timestamp. In case the file does not exist yet, an empty file will be created that has the current timestamp (see image below).

```
user@debian95: ~
File  Edit  View  Search  Terminal  Help
user@debian95:~$ touch testfile
user@debian95:~$ ls -la testfile
-rw-r--r-- 1 user user 0 Aug  6 13:35 testfile
user@debian95:~$
```

Use the touch command in order to set the
timestamp of a file and to figure out if you have the
appropriate permissions to write to a directory or an
entire filesystem.

ls

This command lists the entries of a directory. The
image below shows two common ways: without any
options, and with the options **-la** (short for -l -a
which means long all). The first output displays the
entry names only for regular files, whereas the
second output lists both regular and hidden entries.
Over and above, it shows all the information like
type of entry, permissions, name of owner, size of
entry, access date and name of entry.

```
                            user@debian95: ~
File  Edit  View  Search  Terminal  Help
user@debian95:~$ ls
Desktop     Downloads   Pictures   Templates   Videos
Documents   Music       Public     testfile
user@debian95:~$ ls -la
total 128
drwxr-xr-x 14 user user   4096 Aug  6 13:35 .
drwxr-xr-x  4 root root   4096 Jul 26 14:00 ..
-rw-------  1 user user     24 Aug  6 11:33 .bash_history
-rw-r--r--  1 user user    220 Jul 26 14:00 .bash_logout
-rw-r--r--  1 user user   3526 Jul 26 14:00 .bashrc
drwxr-xr-x  6 user user   4096 Aug  6 09:54 .cache
drwx------ 10 user user   4096 Aug  6 11:37 .config
drwxr-xr-x  2 user user   4096 Jul 26 14:34 Desktop
drwxr-xr-x  2 user user   4096 Jul 26 14:34 Documents
drwxr-xr-x  2 user user   4096 Jul 26 14:34 Downloads
drwx------  3 user user   4096 Jul 26 14:34 .gnupg
-rw-------  1 user user    644 Aug  6 09:45 .ICEauthority
drwxr-xr-x  3 user user   4096 Jul 26 14:34 .local
drwxr-xr-x  2 user user   4096 Jul 26 14:34 Music
drwxr-xr-x  2 user user   4096 Jul 26 14:34 Pictures
-rw-r--r--  1 user user    675 Jul 26 14:00 .profile
drwxr-xr-x  2 user user   4096 Jul 26 14:34 Public
drwxr-xr-x  2 user user   4096 Jul 26 14:34 Templates
-rw-r--r--  1 user user      0 Aug  6 13:35 testfile
drwxr-xr-x  2 user user   4096 Jul 26 14:34 Videos
-rw-------  1 user user    163 Aug  6 09:45 .Xauthority
-rw-r--r--  1 user user  12102 Aug  6 09:45 .xfce4-session.verbose-log
-rw-r--r--  1 user user  14861 Aug  5 09:30 .xfce4-session.verbose-log.last
-rw-------  1 user user  18192 Aug  6 13:36 .xsession-errors
user@debian95:~$ █
```

In order to list directories only, use the option **-d**
(abbreviates --directory).

mkdir

This command is used in order to create a directory
(make directory). The following example creates a
new directory named "training" in the current
directory:

```
$ mkdir training

$
```

rmdir

This command is used in order to remove an empty directory (remove directory). The following example deletes an empty directory named "training" in the current directory.

```
$ rmdir training

$
```

rm

This command abbreviates the word "remove" and deletes files and directories. In order to delete all the files ending with **.txt** that reside in the current directory issue the following command:

```
$ rm *.txt

$
```

In order to be on the safe side when deleting files and directories, use the option **-i** (or --interactive) in combination with **-v** (for --verbose). Before deleting a file **rm** will then request your explicit confirmation, and prints a status message:

```
$ rm -iv invoice156.txt

rm: remove regular file "invoice156.txt"? y

"invoice156.txt" was deleted

$
```

cp

The **cp** command copies files. In order to operate properly, it requires two names: the name of the original file and the name of the copy. The next example creates a copy of the calendar file that is named "calendar-2018".

```
$ cp calendar calendar-2018

$
```

The original file is not touched and stays intact. The copy has the same content as the original, but with

the current timestamp. Use the option **-i** (or --
interactive) to prevent overwriting existing files.

mv

The **mv** command abbreviates the word "move" and
moves and renames files and directories. It requires
two names: the name of the original file and its new
name. The following example renames the "calendar"
file to "calendar-2018".

```
$ mv calendar calendar-2018
$
```

The original file is removed, and the new entry
receives the current timestamp. Use the option **-i** (or
--interactive) to prevent overwriting existing files.

cd

The **cd** (change directory) command allows you to
move through the system. To move into the
subdirectory "work", use this command:

```
$ cd work

$
```

file

This command also detects PDF files as well as
various image formats.

```
user@debian95: ~
File  Edit  View  Search  Terminal  Help
user@debian95:~$ ls
Desktop      Downloads   Pictures   Templates   Videos
Documents    Music       Public     testfile
user@debian95:~$ file Music
Music: directory
user@debian95:~$ file testfile
testfile: empty
user@debian95:~$ file /etc/passwd
/etc/passwd: ASCII text
user@debian95:~$
```

du and df

These two very similar commands tell you more
about the disk space that is in use, **du** abbreviates
"disk usage" and **df** means "disk free".

du calculates the amount of disk space that is used
by a directory. The regular output states the value
for every single entry and can be a bit confusing. In
order to get a summary for a directory, extend the

command line call by the three parameters **-s**, **-c** and **-h**. **-s** abbreviates "summary", **-c** means "total" and **-h** outputs the value in human-readable format. The image below shows the disk usage of your home directory.

In contrast, the **df** command shows how much space is left on the devices. The image below shows the available disk space of your system. From left to right the columns cover the filesystem, the disk size, the amount of space that is used, the amount of space that is still available and the device that is mounted to that directory.

```
                                    user@debian95: ~
File   Edit   View   Search   Terminal   Help
user@debian95:~$ df -h
Filesystem      Size  Used Avail Use% Mounted on
udev            1.5G     0  1.5G   0% /dev
tmpfs           309M  4.4M  305M   2% /run
/dev/sda1       2.8G  1.9G  741M  72% /
tmpfs           1.6G     0  1.6G   0% /dev/shm
tmpfs           5.0M     0  5.0M   0% /run/lock
tmpfs           1.6G     0  1.6G   0% /sys/fs/cgroup
/dev/sda7       280M  2.1M  259M   1% /tmp
/dev/sda5       1.2G  575M  570M  51% /var
/dev/sda8       7.4G   36M  7.0G   1% /home
tmpfs           309M   12K  309M   1% /run/user/1000
user@debian95:~$
```

7.2 Output and Text Processing

echo

echo is a built-in shell command and is intended to output text:

```
$ echo help

help

$
```

As already shown earlier, the shell evaluates the command and prints the value of variables too. The next example prints the value of the shell variable **$HOME** which represents your home directory.

```
$ echo $HOME

/home/user

$
```

cat and tac

These two commands print a file, line by line. **cat** starts with the first line up to the last line, and **tac** starts with the last line up to the first line. The next example uses a simple plain text file named "places" that contains the names of one city per line. For **cat** Amsterdam comes first, and for **tac** it is Cape Town.

```
$ cat places

Amsterdam

Berlin

Bern

Cape Town

$ tac places

Cape Town

Bern

Berlin

Amsterdam

$
```

grep

Based on the example used above for **cat** and **tac**, the following command line call only outputs the lines from the file that contain the character string "Ber". Keep in mind that **grep** filters are case-sensitive, i.e. it looks for the character string that starts with an uppercase "B" followed by the two lowercase letters "e" and "r". It does not matter whether the pattern is at the beginning, in the middle or at the end of text.

```
$ grep Ber places

Berlin

Bern

$
```

When it comes to patterns, **grep** supports character strings and regular expressions (RegEx). In order to find all the strings that end with the letter "n" use the option **-E** (or --extended-regexp) followed by the pattern "n$" as shown below:

```
$ grep -E "n$" places

Berlin

Bern

Cape Town

$
```

head and tail

head outputs the first lines from a file. Invoked without further parameters it outputs up to ten lines. In contrast **tail** does the same thing but starts at the end of a file. In order to output the first two lines, add the option **-n 2** as follows:

```
$ head -n 2 places

Amsterdam

Berlin

$
```

In order to output the last two lines, do the same thing using **tail** as follows. In contrast to **tac** (see earlier in this chapter) **tail** does not change the order of output.

```
$ tail -n 2 places

Bern

Cape Town
```

```
$
```

nl

nl is similar to **cat** (see earlier in this chapter) but adds a line number at the beginning of each line of output.

```
$ nl places
     1 Amsterdam

     2 Berlin

     3 Bern

     4 Cape Town
$
```

wc

This command abbreviates the phrase "word count" and counts lines, words and single characters of the input data. Unless otherwise specified, all three values are printed:

```
$ wc places
```

```
4  5 32 places

$
```

Amongst others **wc** offers the following options to limit the output:

-l: output the number of lines only, followed by the filename

-w: output the number of words only, followed by the filename

-c: output the number of characters only, followed by the filename

This example shows how to count only the lines in a file:

```
$ wc -l places

 4 places

$
```

7.3 Users and Groups

These commands deal with a variety of actions in order to manage the users and groups of your Linux system. Unless explicitly stated, these commands can be run as a regular user.

whoami

This command returns your current user ID as follows:

```
$ whoami

user

$
```

users, who and w

The **users**, **who** and the **w** commands show the users that are currently logged into your Linux system. **w** extends the output of **who** by the uptime information and another column that contains the last command that was executed. In contrast, **users** simply outputs the name of the users as a space-separated list in a single line (see image below).

The single columns for **who** start with the login name of the user. The output is followed by the name of the terminal, where "console" represents a login terminal, and "pts/1" abbreviates the first pseudo terminal session. The last two columns contain the login time and the host the user comes from, in brackets (see image below).

The single columns for **w** contain the login name of the user (titled LOGIN), the name of the terminal (titled TTY), the name of the host the user comes from (titled FROM), the login time (titled LOGIN@), the activity (idle time and CPU usage titled IDLE, JCPU, and PCPU) as well as the last command the user executed (titled WHAT) (see image below).

```
                              user@debian95: ~                          ⌄ _ □ ✕
File  Edit  View  Search  Terminal  Help
user@debian95:~$ w
 09:49:23 up 9 min,  3 users,  load average: 0.15, 0.03, 0.01
USER      TTY      FROM            LOGIN@   IDLE   JCPU   PCPU WHAT
user      console  :0              09:36    13:14  0.00s  0.04s -:0
user      pts/2    :0              09:47    2:03   0.02s  0.02s xterm
user      pts/3    :0              09:47    2:03   0.01s  0.01s bash
user@debian95:~$ ▌
```

id and groups

The **id** command outputs the user and group information of the current user (see image below). From left to right the columns show the user ID (uid=1000(user)), the group id (gid=1000(group)) and the name of the groups the user is a member of.

In order to list the names of all the groups the user belongs to, you can also invoke the **groups** command (see image below). The output is a space-separated list of the group names.

```
user@debian95: ~
File  Edit  View  Search  Terminal  Help
user@debian95:~$ groups
user cdrom floppy audio dip video plugdev netdev bluetooth
user@debian95:~$
```

passwd

As described in Chapter 4, the Linux system has at least two users: an administrative root user and a regular user that we simply called **user**. Every account is also secured with a password.

In order to change your password, use the **passwd** command from the Debian "passwd" package (refer to Chapter 4 on how to install additional software). As shown below, type in the current password first, press Enter, type in the new password, press Enter to confirm, retype the new password and press Enter to confirm, again.

As a regular user, you are allowed to change your own password only.

The password is stored as a hashed value in the configuration file "/etc/shadow". The content of this file is only visible to the administrative user. The example below shows how to extract the information for the user "user" with the help of the **grep** command (see earlier in this chapter).

chfn

This command is also from the Debian "passwd" package and changes the user information that is stored on your system in the file /etc/passwd. During the installation of your Debian system the basic setup was already done. In order to modify this information, you can run **chfn** without further parameters in interactive mode, or with one or more of the following options to adapt only a specific value:

-f or --full-name: change the full name of the user

-h or --home-phone: change the home phone of the user

-r or --room: change the room number of the user

-w or --work-phone: change the work phone of the user

The following example changes the entry for the home phone number to 135:

```
$ chfn -h 135

Password:

$
```

chsh

This command (also from the Debian "passwd" package) changes the entry for the shell that you use to log into your Linux system. Again, this information is stored in the file /etc/passwd. Which shells are allowed to be used are limited by the entries in the configuration file /etc/shells.

chsh works similar to the **chfn** command. Invoked without further options an interactive method is used (see image below).

chsh accepts the option **-s** (short for --shell) in order to set the shell in non-interactive mode. The following example shows the according command line call:

```
$ chsh -s /bin/bash

$
```

In order to modify the shell for a different user other than yourself, invoke the **chsh** command with the username as a parameter. Note that only the administrative user can do this for a different user. The next example shows how to do that for the user "felix".

```
# chsh felix

Changing the login shell for felix

Enter the new value, or press ENTER for the new value

        Login shell [/bin/bash]:

#
```

su and sudo

In order to change your role from one user to another, you utilize the **su** command. **su** abbreviates "switch user". Invoked without further options you change to the root user as follows:

```
$ su

Password:
```

```
#
```

Working as the administrative root user comes with great responsibility and presumes that you know exactly what you are doing. To work as a different user than root, invoke the **su** command with the desired username as follows:

```
$ su felix
Password:
$
```

The **su** command changes the current role permanently. In order to run only a single command as an administrative user, use the **sudo** command. This requires the Debian "sudo" package to be installed (refer to Chapter 4 on installing additional software) and the additional user to be added to the configuration file /etc/sudoers using the **visudo** command. This step will be explained in further detail later on.

adduser

The command **adduser** creates new user accounts. The image below shows the information that is required. This includes a new entry in the file /etc/passwd as well as the creation of a new group, plus home directory. Furthermore, prepared data from the directory /etc/skel is copied into the previously created home directory. Afterward, the account information is modified using the **chsh** command (see earlier in this chapter).

```
                        user@debian95: ~
File  Edit  View  Search  Terminal  Help
root@debian95:~# adduser caro
Adding user `caro' ...
Adding new group `caro' (1002) ...
Adding new user `caro' (1002) with group `caro' ...
Creating home directory `/home/caro' ...
Copying files from `/etc/skel' ...
Enter new UNIX password:                          I
Retype new UNIX password:
passwd: password updated successfully
Changing the user information for caro
Enter the new value, or press ENTER for the default
        Full Name []: Caro
        Room Number []:
        Work Phone []:
        Home Phone []:
        Other []:
Is the information correct? [Y/n] y
root@debian95:~# █
```

Having set up the new user, the entry in the file /etc/passwd looks as follows:

```
user@debian95: ~
File  Edit  View  Search  Terminal  Help
root@debian95:~# grep caro /etc/passwd
caro:x:1002:1002:Caro,,,:/home/caro:/bin/bash
root@debian95:~#
```

Deleting user accounts and modifying user accounts
is done with the help of the two commands **deluser**
and **usermod**. The usage of these commands will be
explained in further detail later on.

7.4 Process Management

ps

This command lists the running processes of your
Linux system. The image below shows the processes
in your current terminal session, where the call **ps
ax** (see the image thereafter) lists all the processes
in your Linux system. The **ps** command has a long
list of options that will be explained later on in more
detail.

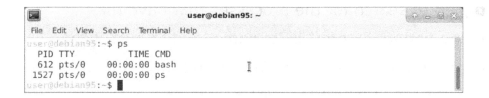

```
                        user@debian95: ~
File   Edit   View   Search   Terminal   Help

user@debian95:~$ ps ax
  PID TTY      STAT   TIME COMMAND
    1 ?        Ss     0:00 /sbin/init
    2 ?        S      0:00 [kthreadd]
    3 ?        S      0:00 [ksoftirqd/0]
    5 ?        S<     0:00 [kworker/0:0H]
    7 ?        S      0:00 [rcu_sched]
    8 ?        S      0:00 [rcu_bh]
    9 ?        S      0:00 [migration/0]
   10 ?        S<     0:00 [lru-add-drain]
   11 ?        S      0:00 [watchdog/0]
   12 ?        S      0:00 [cpuhp/0]
   13 ?        S      0:00 [kdevtmpfs]
   14 ?        S<     0:00 [netns]
   15 ?        S      0:00 [khungtaskd]
   16 ?        S      0:00 [oom_reaper]
   17 ?        S<     0:00 [writeback]
   18 ?        S      0:00 [kcompactd0]
   19 ?        SN     0:00 [ksmd]
   20 ?        SN     0:00 [khugepaged]
   21 ?        S<     0:00 [crypto]
   22 ?        S<     0:00 [kintegrityd]
   23 ?        S<     0:00 [bioset]
   24 ?        S<     0:00 [kblockd]
   26 ?        S<     0:00 [devfreq_wq]
   27 ?        S<     0:00 [watchdogd]
```

pgrep

pgrep is the **grep** command (see earlier in this chapter) for processes. This command looks through the currently running processes and outputs the process ID's that match the given pattern.

The image below shows two calls. The first call asks **pgrep** to search for the processes that have the string pattern "xterm" in its name, and to output the resulting process ID only. The second call uses the two options **-l** (short for --list-name) and **-a** (short for --list-full) in order to show the process ID and the resulting process name.

140

```
user@debian95: ~

File  Edit  View  Search  Terminal  Help
user@debian95:~$ pgrep xterm
741
749
user@debian95:~$ pgrep -la xterm
741 xterm
749 xterm
user@debian95:~$
```

kill

This command sends a specific signal to a process.
In order to terminate this process use the **SIGTERM**
signal. The next example shows how to end the
process that has the process ID 12345.

The command **kill** requires a process ID to work
properly. Use **ps** or **pgrep** to obtain the according
process ID first (see earlier in this chapter).

```
$ kill 12345

$
```

killall

This command is part of the essential Debian
package "psmisc" (refer to Chapter 4 on installing
additional packages). **killall** sends a signal to all the
processes that match the specified command. As an
example, the command

```
killall firefox
```

sends the signal **SIGTERM** to all the processes that have the name "firefox" in order to terminate the process. Amongst other options, **killall** allows these parameters:

-e (short for --exact): require an exact match

-I (short for --ignore-case): treat the process name case-insensitive

-i (short for --interactive): interactively ask for confirmation before terminating the process

-v (short for --verbose): send a confirmation message if the process terminated

The following example shows how to combine the two commands **pgrep** and **killall**. First, obtain the process ID using **pgrep** as well as the exact name of the process. Second, invoke **killall** with the two options **-i** and **-v** to terminate all the processes that have that name. Prior to killing the processes **killall** asks you for confirmation, and afterward outputs a confirmation message.

```
                          user@debian95: ~
File  Edit  View  Search  Terminal  Help
user@debian95:~$ pgrep -la firefox
778 firefox-esr
user@debian95:~$ killall -i -v firefox-esr
Kill firefox-esr(778) ? (y/N) y
Killed firefox-esr(778) with signal 15        I
user@debian95:~$ ▮
```

pkill

The two commands **pkill** and **pgrep** (see earlier in
this chapter) belong to the same software package.
Whilst **pgrep** scans the process list and outputs the
process ID, the **pkill** command will send the
termination signal to the processes that match the
given pattern. In order to terminate all the "xterm"
processes, invoke the following command:

```
$ pkill xterm

$
```

top

The **top** command displays the processes according
to their activity. The most active process is on top,
followed by the less active ones. The list is updated
every second. The single columns contain the
process ID (titled PID), the username of the owner

of the process (titled USER), the process priority (titled PR), the nice level (titled NI), the virtual memory usage (titled VIRT), the reserved memory (titled RES), the shared memory (titled SHR), both the percentile CPU and memory usage (titled %CPU and %MEM), the running time of the process (titled TIME+) as well as the command that was used to invoke the process (titled COMMAND).

In order to quit **top** press the **q** key.

```
                         user@debian95: ~
File  Edit  View  Search  Terminal  Help
top - 06:12:33 up 20:32,  1 user,  load average: 0.02, 0.12, 0.09
Tasks: 104 total,   1 running, 103 sleeping,   0 stopped,   0 zombie
%Cpu(s):  0.0 us,  0.3 sy,  0.0 ni, 99.7 id,  0.0 wa,  0.0 hi,  0.0 si,  0.0 st
KiB Mem :  3159532 total,  2507520 free,   178988 used,   473024 buff/cache
KiB Swap:  3220476 total,  3220476 free,        0 used.  2825480 avail Mem

  PID USER      PR  NI    VIRT    RES    SHR S %CPU %MEM     TIME+ COMMAND
  370 root      20   0  380992  74440  30656 S  0.3  2.4 101:36.61 Xorg
 2441 user      20   0   44888   3760   3156 R  0.3  0.1   0:00.03 top
    1 root      20   0   57140   6836   5248 S  0.0  0.2   0:01.00 systemd
    2 root      20   0       0      0      0 S  0.0  0.0   0:00.00 kthreadd
    3 root      20   0       0      0      0 S  0.0  0.0   0:00.20 ksoftirqd/0
    5 root       0 -20       0      0      0 S  0.0  0.0   0:00.00 kworker/0:0H
    7 root      20   0       0      0      0 S  0.0  0.0   0:00.33 rcu_sched
    8 root      20   0       0      0      0 S  0.0  0.0   0:00.00 rcu_bh
    9 root      rt   0       0      0      0 S  0.0  0.0   0:00.00 migration/0
   10 root       0 -20       0      0      0 S  0.0  0.0   0:00.00 lru-add-dra+
   11 root      rt   0       0      0      0 S  0.0  0.0   0:00.41 watchdog/0
   12 root      20   0       0      0      0 S  0.0  0.0   0:00.00 cpuhp/0
   13 root      20   0       0      0      0 S  0.0  0.0   0:00.00 kdevtmpfs
   14 root       0 -20       0      0      0 S  0.0  0.0   0:00.00 netns
   15 root      20   0       0      0      0 S  0.0  0.0   0:00.02 khungtaskd
   16 root      20   0       0      0      0 S  0.0  0.0   0:00.00 oom_reaper
   17 root       0 -20       0      0      0 S  0.0  0.0   0:00.00 writeback
```

htop

"htop" is an additional software package (refer to Chapter 4 on installing additional packages) and contains a more interactive version of **top** (which we mentioned above). The arrangement of the columns is similar to **top**. Use the navigation and function keys in order to select the processes, sort them, or delete them. The function keys are:

F1: show help

F2: configure htop

F3: search within the process list

F4: filter the terminal output

F5: display the processes as a process tree

F6: change the sort order of the processes

F7: decrease the nice level of the selected process

F8: increase the nice level of the selected process

F9: terminate the selected process

F10: quit the program

```
                              user@debian95: ~
File  Edit  View  Search  Terminal  Help

  CPU[                        0.0%]   Tasks: 53, 55 thr; 1 running
  Mem[|||||||||        182M/3.01G]   Load average: 0.00 0.01 0.04
  Swp[                  0K/3.07G]    Uptime: 20:41:03

  PID USER      PRI  NI  VIRT   RES   SHR S CPU% MEM%   TIME+   Command
  370 root       20   0  372M 74440 30656 S  0.0  2.4  1h41:38 /usr/lib/xorg/Xor
 2606 user       20   0 24448  3696  3168 R  0.0  0.1  0:00.05 htop
  606 user       20   0  616M 36344 26504 S  0.0  1.2  0:04.65 /usr/lib/gnome-te
    1 root       20   0 57140  6836  5248 S  0.0  0.2  0:01.00 /sbin/init
  158 root       20   0 41972  5028  4484 S  0.0  0.2  0:00.49 /lib/systemd/syst
  183 root       20   0 46312  4112  2908 S  0.0  0.1  0:00.17 /lib/systemd/syst
  317 systemd-t  20   0  124M  4136  3644 S  0.0  0.1  0:00.00 /lib/systemd/syst
  293 systemd-t  20   0  124M  4136  3644 S  0.0  0.1  0:00.13 /lib/systemd/syst
  328 root       20   0  244M  3036  2544 S  0.0  0.1  0:00.00 /usr/sbin/rsyslog
  329 root       20   0  244M  3036  2544 S  0.0  0.1  0:00.00 /usr/sbin/rsyslog
  330 root       20   0  244M  3036  2544 S  0.0  0.1  0:00.02 /usr/sbin/rsyslog
  306 root       20   0  244M  3036  2544 S  0.0  0.1  0:00.04 /usr/sbin/rsyslog
  307 root       20   0 29664  2780  2496 S  0.0  0.1  0:00.10 /usr/sbin/cron -f
  309 root       20   0 46500  4780  4196 S  0.0  0.2  0:00.15 /lib/systemd/syst
  331 rtkit      20   0  181M  3072  2764 S  0.0  0.1  0:00.39 /usr/lib/rtkit/rt
  332 rtkit      RT   1  181M  3072  2764 S  0.0  0.1  0:00.16 /usr/lib/rtkit/rt
  310 rtkit      21   1  181M  3072  2764 S  0.0  0.1  0:00.56 /usr/lib/rtkit/rt
F1Help  F2Setup F3SearchF4FilterF5Tree  F6SortByF7Nice  F8Nice +F9Kill  F10Quit
```

7.5 Network and System Information

uname

uname abbreviates the term "UNIX name". The command displays system information such as the exact name and version of the Linux kernel and the hostname of your computer.

The image below shows the call of the **uname** command with the parameter **-a** (short for --all). The output contains the name of the operating system (Linux), the hostname (debian95), the kernel version and its build date (4.9.8-7-amd64 #1 SMP

Debian 4.9.110-1 (2018-07-05)) as well as the architecture of the system (x86_64).

```
                        user@debian95: ~
File  Edit  View  Search  Terminal  Help
user@debian95:~$ uname -a
Linux debian95 4.9.0-7-amd64 #1 SMP Debian 4.9.110-1 (2018-07-05) x86_64 GNU/Linux
user@debian95:~$
```

uptime

This command shows how long the system is running. It displays the current time (07:36:47) followed by the uptime in hours (21:56), the number of logged in users (1 user) and the average load (load average: 0.47, 0.43, 0.29) for the last 1, 5 and 15 minutes.

```
                        user@debian95: ~
File  Edit  View  Search  Terminal  Help
user@debian95:~$ uptime
 07:36:47 up 21:56,  1 user,  load average: 0.47, 0.43, 0.29
user@debian95:~$
```

In order to see the **uptime** in a nicer way, use the option **-p** (short for --pretty). The image below displays a more human-readable version of the information. The system is up 22 hours and 3 minutes.

```
                        user@debian95: ~
File  Edit  View  Search  Terminal  Help
user@debian95:~$ uptime -p
up 22 hours, 3 minutes
user@debian95:~$
```

ip

The **ip** command (along with the two keywords **address show**) displays the current network configuration. The image below shows the loopback interface (lo) and the ethernet interface (enp0s3). The ethernet interface is configured with the IP address 10.0.2.15. The network interfaces are abbreviated as follows:

lo: the loopback interface. It is used to access local services such as a proxy or web server http://127.0.0.1/

eth0: the first Ethernet interface connected to a network switch or router

wlan0: the first wireless interface

```
                            user@debian95: ~
File  Edit  View  Search  Terminal  Help
user@debian95:~$ ip address show
1: lo: <LOOPBACK,UP,LOWER_UP> mtu 65536 qdisc noqueue state UNKNOWN group default q
len 1
    link/loopback 00:00:00:00:00:00 brd 00:00:00:00:00:00
    inet 127.0.0.1/8 scope host lo
       valid_lft forever preferred_lft forever
    inet6 ::1/128 scope host
       valid_lft forever preferred_lft forever
2: enp0s3: <BROADCAST,MULTICAST,UP,LOWER_UP> mtu 1500 qdisc pfifo_fast state UP gro
up default qlen 1000
    link/ether 08:00:27:e3:5c:79 brd ff:ff:ff:ff:ff:ff
    inet 10.0.2.15/24 brd 10.0.2.255 scope global enp0s3
       valid_lft forever preferred_lft forever
    inet6 fe80::a00:27ff:fee3:5c79/64 scope link
       valid_lft forever preferred_lft forever
user@debian95:~$
```

ping

ping sends ICMP network packets to the given IP address or hostname and displays the turnaround time. The image below demonstrates this for the host **http://www.google.com**.

```
user@debian95: ~
File  Edit  View  Search  Terminal  Help
user@debian95:~$ ping google.com
PING google.com (172.217.23.142) 56(84) bytes of data.
64 bytes from fra16s18-in-f14.1e100.net (172.217.23.142): icmp_seq=1 ttl=63 time=36
.9 ms
64 bytes from fra16s18-in-f14.1e100.net (172.217.23.142): icmp_seq=2 ttl=63 time=37
.9 ms
64 bytes from fra16s18-in-f14.1e100.net (172.217.23.142): icmp_seq=3 ttl=63 time=40
.1 ms
^C
--- google.com ping statistics ---
3 packets transmitted, 3 received, 0% packet loss, time 2003ms
rtt min/avg/max/mdev = 36.953/38.353/40.193/1.377 ms
user@debian95:~$
```

How did we do?

Did we meet your expectations? My wife and I put a lot of effort into this guide, spending many late nights adding examples and tweaking formats, and would love to get your genuine feedback on what you thought about it. Leave us a short review on Amazon and tell us: What were your expectations when you bought this guide? Did we live up to them? What would you change? What other guides would you want to see?

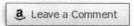

net-tools

Echo

This command will help you move some data, usually in text form into a file. For instance, if you want to add to another that is already made or make a new text file altogether, all you have to do is simply enter:

'echo hello, my name is alok>> new.txt'.

Here, you don't need to use the backward slash to separate the spaces because you'll add two triangle brackets when you complete what you need to write.

Cat

This command is used to display file contents. You'll find it important when you want to view programs easily.

```
nayso@Alok-Aspire:~/Desktop$ echo hello, my name is alok >> new.txt
nayso@Alok-Aspire:~/Desktop$ cat new.txt
hello, my name is alok
nayso@Alok-Aspire:~/Desktop$ echo this is another line >> new.txt
nayso@Alok-Aspire:~/Desktop$ cat new.txt
hello, my name is alok
this is another line
```

Nano, jed, vi

First of all, the command 'nano' is a great text editor that denotes the colored keywords, besides being able to recognize most languages. Vi on the other hand is simpler than nano. You can make a new file or use the editor to modify a file. Let's take an example.

You want to make a file with the name 'check.txt'. You can use the 'nano check.txt' command to make it.

After editing, you can save the files with the sequence ctrl+x, and then y (yes) or n (no).

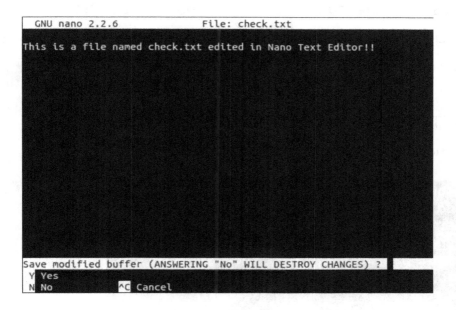

Sudo

'sudo' means 'super user do'. That means that if you want to have any command implemented with root or administrative privileges, you can invoke the 'sudo' command.

Let's take an example:

You want to edit the file 'viz. Alsa-base.conf' or any other file that requires root permission. You can use the following command:

'sudo nano alsa-base.conf'

You can use the 'sudo bash' command to enter the root command line, and then enter your user password. Another command you can use to do this is 'su', but you'll have to set a root password before that. To do that, you can enter the 'sudo passwd' command and then enter the new password.

```
nayso@Alok-Aspire:~/Desktop$ sudo passwd
[sudo] password for nayso:
Enter new UNIX password:
Retype new UNIX password:
passwd: password updated successfully
nayso@Alok-Aspire:~/Desktop$ su
Password:
root@Alok-Aspire:/home/nayso/Desktop# █
```

Df

If you want to see how much disk space you have left in each of your system's partitions, you can use the 'df' command. All you have to do is type it in your command line and you'll be able to see each mounted partition and how much space is used or available in kilobytes. You can use the command 'df -m' if you want to see it displayed in megabytes.

```
root@Alok-Aspire:/home/nayso/Desktop# df -m
Filesystem     1M-blocks  Used Available Use% Mounted on
udev                 940     1       940   1% /dev
tmpfs                191     2       189   1% /run
/dev/sda5          96398 23466     68013  26% /
none                   1     0         1   0% /sys/fs/cgroup
none                   5     0         5   0% /run/lock
none                 951     1       950   1% /run/shm
none                 100     1       100   1% /run/user
```

Tar

This command is useful when you want to work with tarballs (archives or files compressed in archives) in the command line. You can use it to do so much; you can use it to compress or un-compress various kinds of tar archives such as .tar.gz, .tar and .tar.bz2. It works based on the arguments you give it. For instance, 'tar -cvf' will create a .tar archive, -xvf will untar a tar archive and –tvf will list the archive's contents. You can take a look at **these** examples of tar commands to learn more.

Zip and unzip

You'll use 'zip' to compress files into a zip archive and 'unzip' to extract them from a zip archive.

Uname

This command helps you see information about the system your distro is running at the moment. To print out the information about the system, you can use the 'uname-a' command. You'll have the kernel release date, processor type, version and so on.

```
nayso@Alok-Aspire:~$ uname -a
Linux Alok-Aspire 4.4.0-22-generic #40~14.04.1-Ubuntu SMP Fri May 13 17:27:18 UT
C 2016 i686 i686 i686 GNU/Linux
```

Apt-get

'apt' comes in when you want to work with packages in Linux. 'apt-get' installs the packages. You'll require root privileges here so you'll have to use the 'sudo' command along with it. For instance, let's say you wish to install the 'jed' text editor. You'll have to type in the following:

'sudo apt-get install jed'

This is how you'll install other packages as well. You'll also want to update the repository whenever you install a brand new package- which is as simple as typing 'sudo apt-get update'. Replace the word 'update' with 'upgrade' to upgrade the distro. Moreover, the 'apt-cache search' command searches for a package.

```
nayso@Alok-Aspire:~$ sudo apt-get install jed
Reading package lists... Done
Building dependency tree
Reading state information... Done
The following extra packages will be installed:
  jed-common libslang2-modules slsh
Suggested packages:
  gpm
The following NEW packages will be installed:
  jed jed-common libslang2-modules slsh
0 upgraded, 4 newly installed, 0 to remove and 419 not upgraded.
Need to get 810 kB of archives.
After this operation, 2,992 kB of additional disk space will be used.
Do you want to continue? [Y/n] █
```

Chmod

When you want to make your file more executable
and change the permissions it is granted by Linux,
'chmod' is your command. You can imagine having a
python code called 'numbers.py' on your computer.
You'll have to run 'python numbers.py' each time
you have to run it. Instead of doing that, you can
simply run the file by running 'numbers.py' in the
terminal. The command 'chmod +x numbers.py' will
help you make the file executable in this case. You
can give it root permissions with 'chmod 755
numbers.py' or, for root executable, sudo chmod +x
numbers.py'.

```
nayso@Alok-Aspire:~/Desktop$ ls
numbers.py
nayso@Alok-Aspire:~/Desktop$ chmod +x numbers.py
nayso@Alok-Aspire:~/Desktop$ ls
numbers.py
```

Hostname

If you want to know the name in your network or host, simply use 'hostname'. It essentially displays your IP address and hostname. If you want to get your network IP address, simply type in 'hostname -i'.

```
nayso@Alok-Aspire:~/Desktop$ hostname
Alok-Aspire
nayso@Alok-Aspire:~/Desktop$ hostname -I
192.168.1.36
```

Ping

This command is great when it comes to checking your connection to a server. For those who are more technically inclined, it is a software utility in computer network administration that you use to test host reachability on an IP network.

Let's take a simple example: when you enter something like 'ping google.com', it checks whether it can connect to the server and come back. This round-trip time is measured and you get the full details about it. People like us however use this command for simple stuff like checking the internet connection.

In our case, if it pings the server (Google), it means your internet connection is active.

```
nayso@Alok-Aspire:~/Desktop$ ping google.com
PING google.com (172.217.26.206) 56(84) bytes of data.
64 bytes from google.com (172.217.26.206): icmp_seq=1 ttl=56 time=51.2 ms
64 bytes from google.com (172.217.26.206): icmp_seq=2 ttl=56 time=47.9 ms
64 bytes from google.com (172.217.26.206): icmp_seq=3 ttl=56 time=48.9 ms
^C
--- google.com ping statistics ---
3 packets transmitted, 3 received, 0% packet loss, time 2000ms
rtt min/avg/max/mdev = 47.959/49.388/51.299/1.417 ms
```

iotop , iftop, hotp

Understanding the execution of a program is essential for being a good system administrator. In this chapter, we will be looking at processes in greater detail, as well as how to work with and manipulate processes. A running instance of a program is known as a process. It is made up of the program instruction, data read from files, as well as other programs or inputs from a system user.

Every process is assigned a Process ID (PID) which allows the system to keep track of all processes. The system boot process has a PID 0, then the initial process has a PID 1, and so on in a sequential manner. The initial process PID 1 refers to /sbin/initd on older Linux systems or /sbin/systemd on contemporary Linux systems.

Working with Processes

ps and pstree

In order to list all the running processes, use either the **ps** command or the **pstree** command.

The output of **ps** as shown above consists of four columns that have the following meanings:

- **PID - the process ID.**

- **TTY - the terminal from which the command was invoked.**

- **TIME - the time the process has been active.**

- **CMD - the command that was invoked.**

The following switches can be used to retrieve additional information regarding the processes:

- **-e and ax: show all processes.**

- **-p: shows information for the given process id only.**

```
$ ps -p 26426
```

```
PID TTY STAT TIME COMMAND

26426 pts/9 Ss 0:00 bash

   $
```

- **-C: shows processes that refer to the given command name.**

- **-u: shows processes that belong to the given username.**

The **pstree** command is similar to the **ps** command but displays the processes as a hierarchical tree. A useful switch is **-p** which adds the process ID to the process name.

```
                              user@debian95: ~
File  Edit  View  Search  Terminal  Help
root@debian95:/home/user# pstree
systemd─┬─agetty
        ├─cron
        ├─dbus-daemon
        ├─dhclient
        ├─polkitd─┬─{gdbus}
        │         └─{gmain}
        ├─pulseaudio─┬─{alsa-sink-Intel}
        │            └─{alsa-source-Int}
        ├─rsyslogd─┬─{in:imklog}
        │          ├─{in:imuxsock}
        │          └─{rs:main Q:Reg}
        ├─rtkit-daemon───2*[{rtkit-daemon}]
        ├─sshd
        ├─systemd─┬─(sd-pam)
        │         ├─at-spi-bus-laun─┬─dbus-daemon
        │         │                 ├─{dconf worker}
        │         │                 ├─{gdbus}
        │         │                 └─{gmain}
        │         ├─at-spi2-registr─┬─{gdbus}
        │         │                 └─{gmain}
        │         ├─dbus-daemon
        │         ├─dconf-service─┬─{gdbus}
        │                         └─{gmain}
```

pidof

The **pidof** command simply displays the ID of the specified process. The image below returns the PID of the processes that run "bash".

pgrep

This command searches the list of processes for the specified process name. The image below displays the processes that match the string "xfce".

```
user@debian95: ~
File  Edit  View  Search  Terminal  Help
root@debian95:/home/user# pgrep -li xfce
489 xfce4-session              I
506 xfce4-panel
root@debian95:/home/user#
```

top

The **top** command displays the processes according to their activity. The most active process is on top, followed by the less active ones. The list is updated every second. The single columns contain the process ID (titled PID), the user name of the owner of the process (titled USER), the process priority (titled PR), the nice level (titled NI), the virtual memory usage (titled VIRT), the reserved memory (titled RES), the shared memory (titled SHR), both the percentile CPU and memory usage (titled %CPU and %MEM), the running time of the process (titled TIME+) as well as the command that was used to invoke the process (titled COMMAND).

```
                            user@debian95: ~
File  Edit  View  Search  Terminal  Help
top - 20:17:35 up 16:16,  1 user,  load average: 0.00, 0.00, 0.00
Tasks: 102 total,   1 running, 101 sleeping,   0 stopped,   0 zombie
%Cpu(s):  1.0 us,  0.0 sy,  0.0 ni, 99.0 id,  0.0 wa,  0.0 hi,  0.0 si,  0.0 st
KiB Mem :  3159532 total,  2590032 free,   162360 used,   407140 buff/cache
KiB Swap:  3220476 total,  3220476 free,        0 used.  2830844 avail Mem

  PID USER      PR  NI    VIRT    RES    SHR S %CPU %MEM     TIME+ COMMAND
  400 root      20   0  368348  61944  29728 S  2.7  2.0  65:32.50 Xorg
  511 user      20   0  490724  37948  21540 S  0.7  1.2   0:02.17 xfdesktop
  503 user      20   0  179300  19828  16552 S  0.3  0.6   0:03.64 xfwm4
  563 user      20   0  220316   5760   5168 S  0.3  0.2   0:00.06 at-spi2-registr
  617 user      20   0  631268  37536  27396 S  0.3  1.2   0:06.22 gnome-terminal-
 2576 user      20   0   44788   3588   3056 R  0.3  0.1   0:00.03 top
    1 root      20   0   56912   6752   5316 S  0.0  0.2   0:01.81 systemd
    2 root      20   0       0      0      0 S  0.0  0.0   0:00.00 kthreadd
    3 root      20   0       0      0      0 S  0.0  0.0   0:00.18 ksoftirqd/0
    5 root       0 -20       0      0      0 S  0.0  0.0   0:00.00 kworker/0:0H
    7 root      20   0       0      0      0 S  0.0  0.0   0:00.23 rcu_sched
    8 root      20   0       0      0      0 S  0.0  0.0   0:00.00 rcu_bh
    9 root      rt   0       0      0      0 S  0.0  0.0   0:00.00 migration/0
   10 root       0 -20       0      0      0 S  0.0  0.0   0:00.00 lru-add-drain
   11 root      rt   0       0      0      0 S  0.0  0.0   0:00.21 watchdog/0
```

htop

"htop" is an additional software package and contains a more interactive version of **top**. The arrangement of the columns is similar to **top**.

```
                              user@debian95: ~
File  Edit  View  Search  Terminal  Help
CPU[                          0.0%]  Tasks: 51, 56 thr; 1 running
Mem[||||||||           176M/3.01G]  Load average: 0.00 0.00 0.00
Swp[                        0K/3.07G]  Uptime: 16:23:52

  PID USER     PRI  NI  VIRT   RES   SHR S CPU% MEM%   TIME+  Command
    1 root      20   0 56912  6752  5316 S  0.0  0.2  0:01.82 /sbin/init
  573 root      20   0  430M  7568  6120 S  0.0  0.2  0:00.08  ├─ /usr/lib/udisks2/udisksd
  578 root      20   0  430M  7568  6120 S  0.0  0.2  0:00.00  │  ├─ /usr/lib/udisks2/udis
  577 root      20   0  430M  7568  6120 S  0.0  0.2  0:00.00  │  ├─ /usr/lib/udisks2/udis
  576 root      20   0  430M  7568  6120 S  0.0  0.2  0:00.00  │  ├─ /usr/lib/udisks2/udis
  574 root      20   0  430M  7568  6120 S  0.0  0.2  0:00.00  │  └─ /usr/lib/udisks2/udis
  552 user       9 -11  362M 11312  8444 S  0.0  0.4  0:00.18  ├─ /usr/bin/pulseaudio --st
  561 user      -6   0  362M 11312  8444 S  0.0  0.4  0:00.02  │  ├─ /usr/bin/pulseaudio -
  560 user      -6   0  362M 11312  8444 S  0.0  0.4  0:00.03  │  └─ /usr/bin/pulseaudio -
  514 root      20   0  303M  8504  7324 S  0.0  0.3  0:00.53  ├─ /usr/lib/upower/upowerd
  521 root      20   0  303M  8504  7324 S  0.0  0.3  0:00.02  │  ├─ /usr/lib/upower/upowe
  520 root      20   0  303M  8504  7324 S  0.0  0.3  0:00.00  │  └─ /usr/lib/upower/upowe
  507 user      20   0  370M 15160 12856 S  0.0  0.5  0:00.95  ├─ xfsettingsd --display :0
  513 user      20   0  370M 15160 12856 S  0.0  0.5  0:00.00  │  ├─ xfsettingsd --display
  512 user      20   0  370M 15160 12856 S  0.0  0.5  0:00.89  │  └─ xfsettingsd --display
F1Help F2Setup F3SearchF4FilterF5SortedF6CollapF7Nice -F8Nice +F9Kill F10Quit
```

Foreground and Background Processes

There are two types of processes: foreground and background processes. Foreground processes are initialized and controlled through a terminal session. In other words, there has to be a user connected to the system to start these processes and the process occupies the terminal while it is executing. In contrast, background processes are not connected to the terminal and do not explicitly require any user input. They hence do not occupy the terminal while waiting to be completed and allow you to run multiple processes.

Processes can be initialized in the background with the use of the "&" symbol.

```
$ process1 &
```

```
...

$
```

To send a running process to the background, use the command **bg** followed by the job ID, while **fg** will send the process to the foreground. You can use the **jobs** command to show the jobs that are currently running and their associated job IDs:

```
$ process1 &

$ process2 &

$ jobs

[1]+ Running process1

[2]- Running process2

    $
```

Stopping and Terminating Processes

In the event that a running program becomes unresponsive and causes load, what can we do to stop it and get rid of it? Luckily, we have a few options that allow us to send a specific signal to the program in order to stop it. The command used in this instance is the **kill** command with a corresponding switch.

In order to terminate and kill a program named "hangingProgram" you will have to identify the program first. You do this by using **pgrep** to find the associated process as follows:

```
$ pgrep hangingProgram

    3167

    $
```

Next, send the identified process the **SIGTERM** signal:

```
$ kill -SIGTERM 3167
```

As an alternative, you may invoke **kill** as follows:

```
$ kill -15 3167
```

Or you may stop the hanging process by pressing CTRL+Z, and then deleting the process using this command:

```
$ kill -SIGKILL 3167
```

As demonstrated above, this command does the
same:

```
$ kill -9 3167
```

Adjusting the Execution Priority of a Process

You can display the nice level of a process using **ps**
as follows:

```
$ ps -o pid,comm,nice -p 1808

PID COMMAND NI

1808 bash 0

    $
```

The first column contains the Process ID (PID), the
second column contains the command, and the third
contains the nice level (NI). As demonstrated in the
example above, the "bash" process with the PID
1808 has a nice level of 0. An existing process' nice
level can be adjusted using the **renice** command. In

order to reduce the nice level of the process above to 10, issue the command below. Keep in mind that only root can apply negative nice values to a process.

```
$ renice 10 -p 1808
```

Understanding processes

A process in Linux (as in UNIX) is a program that runs in a separate virtual address space. When a user logs into the system, a process is automatically created in which the shell is executed, for example, / bin / bash.

Linux supports the classic multiprogramming scheme. Linux supports parallel (or quasi-parallel if there is only one processor) user processes. Each process runs in its own virtual address space, i.e. processes are protected from each other and the collapse of one process will not affect the other running processes and the system as a whole. One process cannot read anything from the memory (or write to it) of another process without the "permission" of another process. Authorized interactions between processes are allowed by the system.

The kernel provides system calls for creating new processes and for managing generated processes. Any program can start executing only if another process starts it or some interruption occurs (for example, an external device interrupt).

In connection with the development of SMP (Symmetric Multiprocessor Architectures), a mechanism of threads or control threads was introduced into the Linux kernel. A thread is a process that runs in virtual memory, used together with other threads of a process that has separate virtual memory.

If the shell encounters a command corresponding to the executable file, the interpreter executes it, starting from the entry point. For C programs, the entry point is a function of main. A running program can also create a process, i.e. run some program and its execution will also begin with the function main.

Two system calls are used to create processes: fork () and exec. fork () creates a new address space that is completely identical to the address space of the main process. After executing this system call, we get two identical processes: the main and the generated ones. The fork () function returns 0 in the spawned process, and the PID (Process ID is the spawn of the spawned process) basically. PID is an integer.

Now that we have already created the process, we can start the program by calling exec. The exec function parameters are the name of the executable file and, if necessary, the parameters that will be passed to this program. A new program will be loaded into the address space of the fork () process and will start from the entry point (the address of the main function).

As an example, consider this fragment of the program.

if (fork () == 0) wait (0);

else execl ("ls", "ls", 0); / * spawned process * /

Now let's take a closer look at what happens when you execute a fork () call:

1. Memory is allocated for the new process handle in the process table.

2. Assign process ID PID.

3. A logical copy of the process is created that performs fork () – full copying of the virtual memory

contents of the parent process, copying the components of the nuclear static and dynamic contexts of the ancestor process.

4. Increase the file opening counters (the child process inherits all open files of the parent process).

5. Returns the PID to the return point from the system call in the parent process and 0 in the descendant process.

General process control scheme.

Each process can spawn a completely identical process using fork (). The parent process can wait until all its descendant processes have completed executing using the wait system call.

At any time, a process can change the contents of its memory image using one of the exec calls types. Each process responds to signals and, of course, can set its own response to signals produced by the operating system. The priority of the process can be changed using the nice system call.

A signal is a way of informing the core process of the occurrence of an event. If several events of the same type occur, only one signal will be sent to the process. A signal means that an event has occurred, but the kernel does not report how many such events have occurred.

Examples of signals:

1. termination of the child process (for example, due to the exit system call (see below))

2. the occurrence of an exceptional situation

3. signals from the user when you press certain keys

You can set the response to a signal by using the signal system call.

func = signal (snum, function);

snum is the signal number, and function is the address of the function to be executed when the specified signal arrives. The return value is the address of the function that will respond to a signal. Instead of function, you can specify zero or one. If a zero was specified, then when the snum signal arrives, the process will be interrupted similarly to the exit call. If you specify a unit, this signal will be ignored, but it is possible

For normal completion of the process call is used.

exit (status);

where status is an integer returned by the ancestor process to inform it about the reasons for the termination of the descendant process.

The exit call can be set at any point in the program, but it can also be implicit, for example, when exiting the main function (when programming in C), the operator return 0 will be interpreted as the system call exit (0);

input / output Redirection

Virtually all operating systems have an input/output redirection mechanism. Linux is no exception to this rule. Usually, programs enter text data from the console (terminal) and output data to the console. When you enter the console means the keyboard, and then output, the terminal display. The keyboard and display are standard input and output (stdin and stdout), respectively. Any input/output can be interpreted as input from a file and output to a file. Work with files is done through their descriptors. UNIX uses three files for input/output: stdin (handle 1), stdout (2), and stderr (3).

The> symbol is used to redirect standard output to a file.

Example:

$ cat> newfile.txt The standard input of the cat command will be redirected to the file newfile.txt, which will be created after the execution of this command. If a file with this name already exists, it will be overwritten. Pressing Ctrl + D will stop the redirect and abort the execution of the cat command.

The <symbol is used to reassign standard command input. For example, if you run the cat <file.txt

command, the file.txt file will be used as standard input, not the keyboard.

The >> symbol is used to append data to the end of the file (append) of the standard command output. For example, unlike the case with the symbol>, the execution of the command cat >> newfile.txt will not overwrite the file if it exists but will add data to its end.

Symbol | is used to redirect the standard output of one program to the standard input of another. For example, ps -ax | grep httpd.

Process Management Commands

Ps command

Designed to display information about running processes. This command has many parameters that you can read about in the manual (man ps). Here I will describe only the most frequently used commands:

⬚ "a" display all processes associated with the terminal (all user processes are displayed)

⬚ "e" show all processes

☐ "t" terminal list, display terminal-related processes

☐ "u" user identifiers, display the processes associated with these identifiers

☐ "g" group IDs, display the processes associated with these group IDs.

☐ "x" display all non-terminal processes

Program "top"

Designed to display information about processes in real time. Processes are sorted by maximum CPU time, but you can change the sort order (see man top).

You can view information about RAM with the help of the free command, and about the disk memory - df. Information about users registered in the system is available using the w command.

Changing process priority useful command

nice [-reduction factor] command [argument]

The nice command executes the specified command with a lower priority, the reduction factor is specified in the range 1..19 (by default it is equal to 10). The superuser can increase the priority of the command. For this you need to specify a negative factor, for example - --10. If you specify a coefficient greater than 19, then it will be considered as 19.

nohup - ignore interrupt signals

nohup command [argument]

nohup runs a command in the ignore mode. Only the SIGHUP and SIGQUIT signals are not ignored.

kill - forced completion of the process

kill [signal number] PID

where PID is the process identifier that can be found using the ps command.

Commands for running processes in the background - jobs, fg, bg

The jobs command lists the processes that run in the background, fg - puts the process in normal mode ("to the foreground" - foreground), and bg - in the background. You can run the program in the background using the <command> &

Chapter 8. Tips and Tricks

Am sure that you are eager and keen to get stuck into more commands and begin doing some actual playing around with the system. We need to cover some theories first before we get into that. When you begin to play around with the system you are able to understand why it is behaving in such a way and you can also be able to learn the commands further.

Creating a Directory

Linux file systems are organized hierarchically. Because data builds up over time with increasing storage capacity, it's necessary to have an efficient and manageable directory structure in order to organize the data. Many people make the mistake of putting all data at the base of the home directory and waste significant amounts of time searching for what they want in the middle of hundreds, if not thousands of files. Set yourself up for a better future by developing the habit of organizing your files into an elegant and efficient file structure now.

Creating a directory is simple. The command to do so is mkdir, short for Make Directory.

mkdir [set of options]

At its simplest, running mkdir and only inputting a directory will create that directory.

pwd

/home/mike

Is

bin Docs public_html

mkdir linuxbookwork

Is

bin Docs linuxbookwork public_html

Let's examine the commands step by step:

Line 1 - First, we ensure that we are in the correct location (my home directory).

Line 2 - List what's already in the directory.

Line 7 - We run the mkdir command and create the directory linuxbookwork (which would be a good place to keep all work related to this book, and keep it separate from all the other files).

It's important to remember that when we supply a directory in this command, we actually are supplying it with a path. Relative or Absolute Path? The following are a few more ways that we can supply a directory to be created.

mkdir /home/mike/anything

mkdir ./something

mkdir ../dir1

mkdir ~/linuxbookwork/dir2

Doesn't make sense? Review chapter 2, Navigation.

There are several options available to mkdir that can be very useful. How can we find out the command line options for a particular command?

First, -p tells mkdir to create parent directories as needed (explained below). The second, -v, has mkdir tell us exactly what it is doing as it does it (as seen above, it usually does not).

mkdir -p linuxbookwork/anything/sample

cd linuxbookwork/anything/sample

pwd

/home/mike/linuxbookwork/anything/sample

Now, the same command with the -v option added.

mkdir -pv linuxbookwork/anything/sample

mkdir: created directory `linuxbookwork/anything'

mkdir: created directory
`linuxbookwork/anything/sample'

cd linuxbookwork/anything/sample

pwd

/home/mike/linuxbookwork/anything/sample

Removing a Directory

It's important though to remember that there is no undo function on the Linux command line (while Linux GUI desktop environment will often include an undo feature, the command line doesn't). Be careful. To remove a directory, the command is rmdir, which is short of remove directory.

rmdir [set of options]

rmdir, like mkdir, supports both the -v and -p options. Additionally, in order to be removed a directory must be empty (there is a way around it, but we will cover that later).

rmdir linuxbookwork/anything/sample

ls linuxbookwork/anything

Blank Files

Many commands that manipulate data within files will actually create files on their own if they are referred to and do not already exist. This characteristic can be used to create blank files, using the command touch.

touch [set of options]

pwd

/home/mike/linuxbookwork

ls

```
foo

touch sample1

ls

sample1 foo
```

The touch command is used to change the access and modification times on a file (generally unnecessary, bus useful when working with a system that relies on file access or modification times). Students will occasional try to use this command to make it appear as though their files were not modified after the due date, though they're rarely successful thanks to ways to detect it. The benefit here is that if we use the command on a file that doesn't exist, it will be automatically created for us.

Using commands and their behavior in creative ways, along with being familiar with different aspects of the system, comprise the main ways that a lot of things are done in Linux.

In the introduction, we mention that the command line provides you with a set of building blocks. Those building blocks can be applied in any way you choose but are most effective when you understand fully how and why each function.

The file we created is blank at the moment. In the future, we will examine methods of inserting and extracting data in and out of files.

Copying a File/Directory

Duplicates of files and directories are useful for a variety of reasons. One of the most common is in order to create a backup version before attempting to make some sort of modification to the original. That way information and progress aren't lost in the event of a mistake. The command to create a duplicate is cp, meaning copy.

cp [set of options]

cp has a wide variety of options available. We'll look at one of them below, but first it's a good idea to look at the main page for cp to see what is available to us.

Is

sample1 foo

cp example 1 barry

Is

barry sample1 foo

In this example, both the source and destrishation are paths, and therefore we can refer to them using both the absolute and relative paths. For example:

cp /home/mike/linuxbookwork/example2 example3

cp example2 ../../mybackups

cp example2 ../../mybackups/example4

cp /home/mike/linuxbookwork/example2 /otherdir/anything/example5

With cp, the destrishation can be either a file or a directory. In the case of a file (examples 1, 3, and 4) it will name the copy of the source by the filename specified in the destrishation. In the case of a directory as the destrishation, it will copy a file of the same name into the specified directory.

By default, cp will only copy an individual file (you can copy multiple files at once, but that will be covered in chapter 6, Wildcards). The -r option, standing for recursive, can be used to copy directories. When you use recursive, you want to look at a directory and all of the files and directories it contains, and subdirectories, and within them do the same thing repetitively.

Is

barry example 1 foo

cp foo something2

cp: omitting directory 'foo'

cp -r foo something2

Is

barry sample1 foo something2

As shown in the example, all of the files and directories in the directory foo will also be copied to something2.

Moving a File or Directory

The mv command is used to move files. mv works a lot like cp, with the slight advantage that it can apply to entire directories without the -r option.

mv [set of options]

ls

barry sample1 foo something2

mkdir mybackups

mv something2 mybackups/anything3

mv barry backsup/

ls

mybackups sample1 foo

Now, to elaborate:

Line 3 - The creation of a new directory, 'mybackups'.

Line 4 - Moving the director something2 into the 'mybackups' directory and rename it something3.

Line 7 - The file barry is moved into mybackups, since no destrishation name was provided, it kept its name.

Keep in mind that the source and also the destrishation are paths and can be referred to as either absolute or relative.

Renaming Files and Directories

Similar to the command touch, the command mv can be used creatively to achieve a different outcome. As shown above on line 4, you can rename a file being moved by providing a new name for the file or directory. If we specify that the destrishation is the same directory as the source, but provide a new name, then mv an effectively rename a file or directory.

Is

mybackups sample1 foo

mv foo something3

Is

mybackups sample1 something3

cd

mkdir Linux bookwork/testdir

mv linuxbookwork/testdir /home/mike/linuxbookwork/fred

Is

187

mybackups sample1 something3 fred

Broken down:

Line 3 - The file foo is renamed something3 (both paths are relative).

Line 6 - Moved into our parent directory. We only do this so that next we can run commands on files and directories that we aren't not currently in the directory of.

Line 8 - The directory testdir is renamed to fred (the source path was relative, and the destrishation absolute).

Removing a File (and Non-Empty Directories)

Like most commands introduced recently, rm has a selection of options to alter how it behaves. You can explore most of them on your own, but one particularly useful one is -r. Just like for cp, -r means recursive. When you use the -r option with the rm command, you can remove directories and all of the files and directories that they hold within them.

Is

mybackups something3 fred

rmdir mybackups

rmdir: failed to remove 'mybackups'. Directory not empty

rm mybackups

rm: cannot remove 'mybackups'. Is a directory

rm -r mybackups

Is

something3 fred

As a safeguard, it's often good to use -i in combination with -r. -i means interactive, when used it will cause a prompt before removing each file and directory, as well as allowing you to cancel the command if need be.

A Command Line Editor

One command line text editor for Linux is known as Vi. As you know, working with the command line is very different from working with a GUI - the command line is just a window with text input and output. Vi works within those limitations and because of that is an incredibly powerful tool. Though intended as a plain text editor, not a word processing suite, it packs a lot more power than both Notepad and Textedit.

Vi is operated entirely by way of the keyboard, the mouse plays no role whatsoever.

The program has two potential modes: insert (input) and edit mode. While in insert mode, you can create content within the file, while in edit mode you can move around within the file as well as actions such as search and replace, copying, deleting, saving, and so on. Generally, people will often mess up by entering commands or trying to input while in the wrong mode. It's fairly easy to recover from either of these mistakes though.

While running vi, it's usually issued with an individual command line argument: the file you want to edit.

vi

In the event that you forget to specify a file, it's best to simply quit vi and restart it. Files specified can have either an absolute or relative path.

Let's have a go at it. It's difficult to demonstrate a lot of the details, so I'll be beginning by listing what you should type, and you can watch what happens.

First, we'll move to the directory that we created back in the file manipulation chapter. We need to create a few new files and don't want them to be mixed up in all of the rest of your files.

Here's how we'll edit our first file:

vi myfirstfile

This command will open the file, and if it doesn't exist it will create it for you and then open it (you don't have to do anything with a file before editing it). In vi, the file will look something like this (though slightly different depending on what kind of system you're on).

~

~

~

~

~

"myfirstfile" [New File]

Vi will always start in edit mode, so now we must switch our mode to insert by pressing the shortcut 'i'. The bottom left corner of the window will indicate which mode you are in.

~

~

~

~

~

--INSERT--

Now you are able to type your lines of text. Pressing esc will return you to edit mode.

Saving and Exiting

In order to save and exit, you've got a few different options that are essentially equivalent. Take your pick. For all, ensure that you begin in edit mode.

Again, if you're unsure which mode you're in, the bottom left corner of the window will indicate it for you. As long as it doesn't read INSERT, you are in edit mode. If you're still not sure, pressing esc will automatically put you into edit mode. Pressing esc while in edit mode already will do nothing.

ZZ (capitalized) - Save and exit.

:q! - Discard all recent changes, save, and exit.

:w - Save the file but keep vi running.

:wq - Save and exit, just like the first option.

Within vi, commands are generally executed as soon as you finish with the sequence of keypresses. If a command begins with a colon (:) you must type a space before it will complete.

Go ahead, save and exit your currently open files.

Conclusion

Linux is an operating system for computers. It exists in various distributions such as Ubuntu, Red Hat, Fedora and Linux mint which are called Linux distros. Each of these distros comes in two versions, that is, the server and the desktop versions.

The sever versions of these distros have no graphics and supports only commands via the command line. This is to ensure a degree of security. This explains why most server computers run Linux as their OS. It also calls for the need to learn and understand the Linux commands. The command line is a very powerful tool in Linux and one can achieve everything that the Graphics users can achieve. Linux users who find themselves comfortable with these commands usually feel proud of it and they earn a great deal of respect in society.

The Linux command line supports numerous commands. These commands can be used to do everything in the system from the time of login to the time of logout or shutdown of the system.

Linux commands can be used to manage files and directories, which is the main purpose with users. Management of files in Linux includes modifying their

194

contents, moving them to other directories, renaming them, as well as creation and deletion of the same files. These tasks can all be achieved via the command line.

Creation of directories, changing of directories, and deletion can also be achieved via the command line. This clearly depicts the power of the Linux command line. Users can also be managed via the command line. This includes adding new users to the system, adding them to particular groups and as well as deletion of the same users from either a group or the system altogether. Managing the network can be done using the command line, including configuring the network for ip addresses, subnet mask and the gateways.